INTERIORS
southeast

leading designers
reveal their most
brilliant spaces

Published by

PANACHE
P A N A C H E   P A R T N E R S

Panache Partners, LLC
1424 Gables Court
Plano, TX 75075
469.246.6060
Fax: 469.246.6062
www.panache.com

Publishers: Brian G. Carabet and John A. Shand

Printed in Malaysia

Distributed by Independent Publishers Group
800.888.4741

PUBLISHER'S DATA

Interiors Southeast

Library of Congress Control Number: 2010940296

ISBN 13: 978-1-933415-97-0
ISBN 10: 1-933415-97-5

First Printing 2011

10 9 8 7 6 5 4 3 2 1

Right: Jackie Naylor Interiors, page 146

Previous Page: Brinson Interiors, page 122

INTERIORS
southeast

introduction

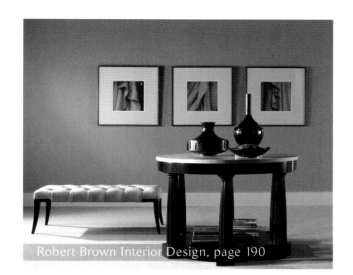

Robert Brown Interior Design, page 190

Cindy Meador Interiors, page 44

Simultaneously exhilarating and formidable, the process of interior design is unlike any other undertaking. To extract the essence that will reflect those living within the home, designers must embark on a journey through the homeowner's life. The process requires knowledge of multiple disciplines, energy and enthusiasm to persevere over time, and a keen ability to understand and communicate with a plethora of personalities.

Interior designers must also take into account the contrasting principles at work in each home: each room needs to have its own flavor yet flow with the rest of the home; the design should be relevant to modern life and still be timeless in aesthetic; and the living space must function as a private sanctuary as well as a haven for entertaining visitors.

Interiors Southeast boasts the impressive work of professionals who effortlessly meet all of the challenges of design, expressing the homeowner's lifestyle and sense of style in ways never even dreamed. This book lays the foundation for inspiration through unparalleled images that present an insider's look into private retreats, and delves even deeper as the experts reveal their philosophies and advice gleaned through years of experience.

Within this extraordinary collection, you'll find hunting sheds turned into lodge-like retreats, high-rise condos transformed from stark to stunning, suburban estates with inspiring views, and weekend cottages that beckon relaxation from everyday life. From the coast to the lake, from the mountains to the cities, these designers passionately redefine what it means to turn a house into a home.

contents

C. Weaks Interiors, page 42

Anita Rankin Interiors, page 18

Todd Richesin Interiors

Todd Richesin begins each new design project by asking a variety of questions to figure out how the home will be used, how each space needs to function, and what aesthetic will strike a chord with the residents. Each of his creations is unique, yet Todd is drawn to rooms that have an understated elegance and an ambience that welcomes guests to make themselves comfortable anywhere in the home. While he certainly enjoys designing in the traditional mountain style, he has developed a "new mountain" look for residents who prefer an unexpected flavor that is still entirely appropriate for the setting.

Above & Facing Page: The homeowners very much wanted a departure from the norm, and I think we achieved it with the use of aqua and orange, which creates a new mountain home look. The effect is light, cozy, and fun. In addition to color, a mix of patterns gives the rooms a lived-in, collected feel. I designed braided rugs to subtly unite the color scheme of the open kitchen and great room. I love the concept of making an old art form feel new, and since braided rugs do exactly that they are an important part of the design. The fabulous breakfast nook is the heart of the home and the owners' favorite space. The cozy draperies make you want to stay in the room reading all day.
Photographs by Dale McGiboney, Highland Mediaworks

Above: In a new house, antique elements lend an instant sense of authenticity. The twisted columns on the refrigerator are antiques, but the rest is brand new. The varied cabinetry and antique buffet with hutch offer a more interesting solution than matching cabinets and give the kitchen the feeling of a space that has grown over time. The result is an authentic European country look.

Facing Page Top: A design project can start in many different ways—a cherished painting, an antique carpet, a passion for a specific genre of furniture, or even a color or two. Because the Highlands Story home's owners liked aqua and orange, I began by selecting fabrics: vividly dyed and patterned crewel, toile, and herringbone. It's an art form to assemble a variety of colors and patterns in a way that makes sense but isn't overwhelming.

Facing Page Bottom: The bedroom continues the color scheme with the use of blue. The antique chest contributes a softer theme in harmony with the main part of the house. A custom rug, an ivory coverlet, and pale blue walls keep the room light and airy. The brown accent creates interest and warmth.
Photographs by Dale McGiboney, Highland Mediaworks

"Comfort is the most important thing about interior design. Beyond the way a chair or sofa sits, it is an emotional thing. A comfortable space entices you to relax."
Todd Richesin

Above: Our design goal was to give the illusion that individual elements in the European country-style home were collected over a lifetime, not all at once. Each piece is interesting, and together they give a collected, comfortable feel as though the home has always existed. The custom iron balcony has Gothic details that are subtly repeated in the fireplace's arch and the iron chandelier. The details on the ceiling add a bit of the Edwardian era to the room, which reads as an interesting and timeless story.

Facing Page Top: Located off the dining room, the screened porch is the perfect entertaining setup. The space is elegant yet casual enough that guests feel welcome to kick up their feet. The deer chandelier addresses the property's location in the mountains. Neutral colors let the furniture recede and allow the stunning view to be the focal point.

Facing Page Bottom: Flanking the fireplace are restored 19th-century windows from a house in Provence. The home was designed around the rose-colored windows, which cast a warm glow without obstructing the view.
Photographs by Dale McGiboney, Highland Mediaworks

Anita Rankin Interiors

Anita Rankin seeks to create spaces that are comfortable and inviting as well as visually pleasing. Her innovative style often includes the addition of a seating area in a kitchen, a multifunctional library in a seldom-used dining area, or antiques interspersed with a variety of fabrics and accessories, all within the framework of the homeowners' distinctive tastes and desires.

Above & Facing Page: Hidden deep in the river bottom adjoining an oxbow lake on land that has been in the homeowner's family for six generations, the home is intended to serve as a usable camp for deer and turkey hunters while providing comfort and beauty for family and friends. The spectacular 24-foot ceilings, abundant stone, and natural wood establish a background for color, pattern, and texture. Because awareness of scale is essential in the large open areas, I used substantial antique pieces, an enormous English antique horn chandelier, and a large tapestry above the stone fireplace. The remaining wall spaces feature mounted wildlife from the surrounding fields and woods.
Photographs by Courtland William Richards

Above, Left, & Facing Page: I envision a room as multiple layers, beginning with the surfaces and textures of the house, then the furniture and fabrics, and finally the accessories: a key layer that is often overlooked. Throughout the hunting lodge, each layer is coordinated with variations on the central design theme to produce a striking effect. Antiques are interspersed with practical pieces capable of withstanding the wear and tear of a hunting camp. In a corner of the living and dining area, an antique, heavily carved server functions as a bar area and is adorned with turkey tail fans. The cabinets in the kitchen and the walls throughout the home are crafted from cypress, while the floors are made of rough-cut heart pine from an old warehouse. Several different stains create depth on the wooden surfaces. The vaulted ceilings called for special attention to lighting. Fixtures such as the rope and iron chandeliers in the dining area coupled with accent lighting of the scissor trusses impart adequate brightness while creating a warm, inviting atmosphere. A number of flexible seating areas ensure that guests will feel welcome even during large gatherings.
Photographs by Courtland William Richards

Brinson Interiors

A home is at once a private retreat, an entertaining locale, and a place where friends and family can enjoy life together. Therefore it must accommodate many uses while also offering the perfect ambience for the homeowner's personality. Through projects ranging from a retreat in the Bahamas to a private Pullman car sidetracked as a country estate guest house to a pied-a-terre in New Orleans, Louisiana, Wayne Brinson Holder, ASID, has perfected the art of simultaneously creating rooms that are primarily functional and beautiful for the homeowner but still pleasing to guests.

Above: A bachelor who played a significant role in Alabama polo needed a warm retreat that reflected his personality. Personal treasures—such as antique books and polo sculptures—and items from his life—like the pair of Argentinean riding boots that we had made into lamps and set atop an antique mahogany server—illustrate the homeowner in a sophisticated, masculine way.

Facing Page: Every detail in the hunting estate's foyer creates a warm, rich environment, from the antique heart pine beams and locally milled heart pine floors to the leather upholstery and the dark antique rugs. The acorn-shaped hanging lantern with its ring of acorns and leaves around the top was one of the first pieces that began the room's creation. We had the cypress bookcase built to fit the space and added small cypress branches—found on the property—along the edge of the shelves for extra detail.
Photographs by Miller Mobley

"The most wonderful fabrics and furnishings are nothing without balance and proportion."
Wayne Holder

Above: A large equestrian estate needed a more masculine ambience, so we interjected a mixture of antiques and hearty rugs and fabrics within the formal paneled library. We reupholstered inherited sofas in Ultrasuede and added a nailhead trim; the formal simplicity complements the wool pillows and their Navajo-inspired pattern. The coyote in the fireplace reflects the homeowner's hunting hobby.

Facing Page: To create a strong focal point for the hunting estate's living room, we worked with the stone mason to design a stacked fireplace that could also be enjoyed from the covered, screened-in porch. Minimal accessories allow the fireplace to speak for itself. A nook just off the living room became a bar featuring an antique English oak server. Throughout the home, we avoided the use of recessed lighting to maintain a traditional feel; the lamps and chandeliers give off a warm glow that beautifully affects the ambience.
Photographs by Miller Mobley

Jackie Naylor Interiors

Armed with the time-honored technique of pencil and paper drawings, Jackie Naylor, ASID, intelligently tackles each project with a firm foundation in established practices. Yet she doesn't just stay with what has worked in the past. Instead, she melds accepted design principles with an unparalleled design intuition, which allows her to explore new techniques and styles to appropriately respond to each homeowner's desires and needs. Nowhere other than in the mountainous regions is the combination of old and new more important; a previously existing feel is needed to blend in with the longstanding surroundings yet innovation is required to capture modern living.

Above & Facing Page: Just because something is recently built doesn't mean that it has to look that way. In order for the log cabin to feel as if it had existed in the forest for many years, I incorporated various elements that gave an aged look: reclaimed wood flooring, old beams, bark used as trim, and old barn wood for cabinets. I was even able to blend upscale finishes in the bathroom and kitchen to respect the historical feel. A concrete sink in the bathroom and concrete countertops in the kitchen allude to past days, as does the kitchen's undermount copper farmhouse sink. A few contemporary touches—stainless appliances, slate bathroom floors, and a mobile kitchen island—animate the spaces.
Photographs by Robert Thien

Above & Facing Page: Each design is a series of steps that lead to discovering new methods and ideas. To give the log cabin an authentic ambience, I suggested that the fireplace be relaced with staggered stones. The installer then suggested we find one large stone to integrate on the mantel surround. This turned out beautifully, and we were able to source an 80-ton stone from the surrounding woods. I was subsequently inspired to continue using local materials, so an artisan crafted the staircase railing out of mountain laurel found on the property. Flea market finds—like the Oriental rug and 150-year-old English leather chairs—combine well with the Native American print on the textured cotton chenille sofa and the hammered coffee table. The rich colors in the design, from the dark stained wood to the deep orange and brown in the furniture, tie everything together and embrace an intimate aura.
Photographs by Robert Thien

LGB Interiors

A home's encompassing environment has an immediate influence on the interior design, if not outright then subtly. In the mountainous regions, where many people enjoy resort homes, the location is chosen specifically for its inherent characteristics. Linda Burnside at LGB Interiors chooses to play off of the locale, bringing in the multitude of textures and the slightly heavier ambience that resides in the mountains. This, however, does not mean that each residence resembles a log cabin; instead Linda works within a delicate balance of incorporating nature, weaving in the homeowner's personality, and then merging that style with functional design elements.

Above & Facing Page: In a townhome overlooking a driving range and incredible mountain scenery, I unassumingly drew in elements of nature. Taking cues from the family's apple farm in Tennessee, I captured an autumnal feel with warm colors and sprinkles of orange-red tones. A repeating leaf pattern in the window treatments, chair arms that resemble paddles, backsplash tiles that feature pinecones and acorns, and a kitchen border mimicking pine needles weave the outdoors into the space. The open-concept living area and kitchen embrace large family gatherings—a huge part of the family's use of the resort home. By maintaining a tone-on-tone scheme in the kitchen with understated finishes, I ensured the gorgeous views outside would take center stage in the design.
Photographs by Robert Clark Photography

Above: My design will often spring from one piece of a homeowner's collection. In the main room of the townhome, the large painting above the stairwell was the springboard. From there, I designed a sophisticated room that again featured apple-inspired colors—gold, cinnamon-red, olive green. The couple loved a stone wall they had seen in another home, so we designed a lovely stone fireplace that extended the width of the room. The coffered ceiling is interspersed with custom lights that are strategically placed to highlight certain elements.

Facing Page: Taking into account each room's functionality, I embraced a masculine feel in the study—where the husband and his two sons often watch golf—and a more feminine atmosphere in the master bedroom. In both spaces, a variety of textures imparts a tactile quality to add coziness. A large leather chair and ottoman and an oversized chenille sofa provide the tall men in the family comfortable places to relax; the heavier textures, even the chenille drapery with beaded trim, speak to the manly qualities of the room. I engendered a clean feeling in the bedroom with minimal clutter and used Ultrasuede fabric on the bed frame and bedspread to establish warmth.
Photographs by Robert Clark Photography

"Lighting is an integral part of design. The proper location and style guarantee the entire space will be aesthetically successful."
Linda Burnside

Lisa Torbett Interiors

Design is undeniably an artistic endeavor, but the best visions still require a process to keep moving forward. Founding owner Lisa Torbett, ASID, and co-owner Dee Simmons, ASID, have mastered the balance between creativity and organization, between thinking outside the box and staying grounded in reality. By brainstorming together on nearly every project, Lisa and Dee use their generational differences to their advantage, utilizing unique perspectives to achieve the necessary co-mingling of light, scale, pattern, texture, and color.

Above: Because of the intrinsic architectural details like the octagon shape and the heavy stained timbers—and its intended use as a gathering place for a family with multiple teenagers—we felt the room needed a casual ambience where family and friends would want to hang out and watch TV. Because of the substantial beams, texture played an important role in balancing the design. Woven shades, sisal carpet, a carved cabinet, distressed and rustic finishes, and iron light fixtures help ground the space.

Facing Page: The vision for the gathering space was an Adirondack atmosphere with cypress walls, a painted and glazed ceiling, and dark stained beams. We brought in mostly antiques with several newer pieces so the room would feel as if it had existed forever. Leather furniture, an antique rug, and multiple patterns with complementary colors add to the collected look.
Photographs by John Umberger

Above & Right: The presence of dark, rustic wood—especially the 100-year-old reclaimed sinker cypress in the bedroom—naturally leans toward a lodge-like feel and imparts architectural detail that corresponds with warm earth tones. Designed as a personal retreat in a hunting plantation residence, the bedroom includes many antiques and new but traditionally inspired fabrics. The grand hall in a second property links one entertaining room to another, drawing guests through the different spaces. At the end of the long corridor, captivating artwork over an antique chest creates a focal point.

Facing Page: The homeowner's fondness for the Old West allowed us to embrace warm colors and geometric patterns next to Native American artifacts in the nine-bedroom, shingled vacation residence. Reclaimed beams from a cotton mill provide excellent texture for the rafters and the wall logs beneath the staircase.
Photographs by John Umberger

Monday's House of Design

Lynn Monday, principal of Monday's House of Design, has created spaces for residents from New York to Florida. Born in diverse Washington, D.C.—which instilled in her a unique appreciation for all cultures—Lynn learned early on how to understand the home's structure and architectural plans, thanks to her father's career as a builder and developer. Other professional development—such as a degree in fine art and experience in the fashion industry—continues to assist her in balancing color and texture and correctly placing accessories, and gives her an in-depth knowledge of fabric. Over time, these traits have melded into designs that are at once pragmatic and elegant.

Above & Facing Page: At Stillwater Farm amidst magnificent gypsy horses, visitors are accommodated in the luxurious guest quarters of an enormous barn. A breezeway with the corral behind offers the perfect space to relax outdoors, while a sitting area inside embodies an elegant, rustic charm; both speak of my penchant for spaces that have a timeless, acquired look.
Photographs by Chris Little Photography

Above, Right & Facing Page: I continued the charming, refined atmosphere upstairs with goose down pillows and fine linens, a spindle bed, an antique dresser, and hand-painted etchings of horses. The sisal rug and cozy window seat add a bit of warmth without being too predictable. I lined and bump-lined fabric for the window treatments to shut out the light and give the drapery a soft roll.
Photographs by Chris Little Photography

C. Weaks Interiors

Color is clearly an important consideration in any interior design. It complements the style, sets the tone, and profoundly influences how people feel. Because sunlight is perceived differently in various geographic locations—it bounces off lush mountainsides as a cool tone yet radiates with intense physical and visual warmth near the equator—Carole Weaks always finalizes her color palette on site. She carefully ensures that the hues perfectly complement the natural setting and of course chooses textiles and furnishings in a similarly location-sensitive manner.

Above: Everything in the living room is oriented to the unbelievable view of nature's art, Whiteside Mountain. The drapery selection works well because it's strong enough to act as a frame but isn't distracting. Plain sheers, as elegant as they look by the beach, would have been completely lost here. Inspired by the homeowners' lifestyle, the space is nice and open and has three different seating areas—one for every mood and occasion.

Facing Page: To complement the antique French bookcase, I designed a pair of substantial walnut tables that are equally ideal for reading, conducting research, gazing out the picture window, and dining. When all two dozen extended family members visit, the tables can be extended and rearranged into a banquet formation to seat everyone quite comfortably.
Photographs by Emily Followill

Cindy Meador Interiors

Designing a home should be a fun, exciting project during which the homeowner enjoys hearing from the designer and looks forward to planning meetings. The relationship between the homeowner and designer should be a symbiotic, copacetic partnership. Impossible? Not when Cindy Meador's in charge. As the unexpected breath of fresh air and the self-proclaimed olive in the martini, Cindy loves her work and makes sure every aspect of the process is as stress-free as possible. This peaceful method culminates in a beautifully distinct home that smartly reflects the homeowner.

Above: Using reclaimed materials in a new home or in a renovation offers many benefits, especially in a mountainous region where nature is all around. In addition to being eco-friendly, reclaimed materials tell a story about the local area. In two separate houses, an architect used all antique heart pine from various places, including trees pulled from a local river for the flooring and wood from an old mill for the cabinets. Despite the similar materials, I allowed each home to exude its own charm. One feels like a high-end lodge while the other gives a nod to Low Country style.

Facing Page: A renovation in an old Tudor home prompted a new addition for the kitchen. Clean lines and stainless steel finishes combine with lots of wood and brick to maintain a hint of the Tudor style but with contemporary flair.
Photographs by Parish Stapleton

Knotting Hill Interiors

The specifics of good design are unique to each home and even each room, yet Kimberly Grigg, founder and principal designer of Knotting Hill Interiors, sees a common element that runs through every beautiful space: an appearance as if the furnishings and adornments evolved over time. Often beginning with the selection of textiles, she then moves on to the furniture and accessories, allowing the space to come to life. With an ambience that makes the room feel rooted, as if every element within truly belongs in the space, Kimberly is able to capture the distinct personalities that will thrive in the residence.

Above & Facing Page: To protect me from the elements while accompanying my husband on his hunting trips, he built a metal shed, which also housed tractors and other equipment. I decided to make the space more comfortable, and the result was a cozy retreat, complete with a sleeping loft in addition to the main bedroom. The painted concrete floor and Savannah stone on the fireplace and countertops are practical, while the rugs, custom bedding, and window treatments add comfort. Elements from the hunting property adorn the rooms: hunting trophies, shelves crafted from trees on the property, and antlers made into lamps, chandeliers, bowl holders, and even a champagne bucket stand.
Photographs by Carl Kerridge Photography

Liza Bryan Interiors

Liza Bryan has always been tuned in to her surroundings. Even at the young age of 10 she was undaunted by the challenge to rearrange her 10-by-10-foot bedroom, which featured two windows, two closets, and two doors. Years of education and experience have refined her approach and taste since then, but her eye for designing a transformative, fresh space still remains. The essential factor in all of her work boils down to appropriate elements, which she analyzes using four tests: visual appeal, correct scale, quality based on price, and usefulness. Liza uses only the furnishings and accessories that pass her inspection to create the classic yet comfortable interiors that reflect the homeowners' lives.

Above & Facing Page: In partnership with Keith Summerour, we crafted a home reminiscent of an aged Canadian lodge with reclaimed quartersawn heart pine floors and beams, locally sourced stone, and furnishings that exude a natural, antique feel. My favorite space is the guest house inglenook because it looks as if the elements were carefully collected over time. An authentic American hooked rug was one of the first selections we made, and it helped lead the tone and sense of the room. The library has incredible bones, so I made sure nothing got in the way of the architecture through a simple palette of brown, ochre, and mustard. Simply because of its size, the main living space presented a challenge. Multiple seating areas and overscaled furniture and accessories, such as the huge chandeliers, generate a cozy, inviting impression.
Photographs by John Umberger

Patricia McLean Interiors, Inc.

With vividly colorful dreams that she is able to remember and then sketch afterwards, it's no wonder that Patricia McLean has taken this ability to memorize and remember specific hues and translated it into her passion for design. Sparked at an early age through her mother and grandmother's own penchant for style and her inclusion in the construction and decoration of a family home, Patricia's design tendencies developed into a fondness for European interiors and classical aesthetics, in part because of her appreciation for art history and Old World craftsmanship—a perfect blending of traits to create exceptional interiors.

Above & Facing Page: The original study in the Cashiers, North Carolina, show house offered a few challenges, including low ceilings and a restriction that the walls could not be altered. Inspired by the lush scenery outside, I commissioned a faux artist to paint screens from photos that I took around the property. Soft, muted colors in the screens, woven wool rug, and floral draperies bring the room to life. Moss and a fern-like plant further soften the abundance of wood and stone. Antique pieces, such as the French daybed and secretary dating back to 1720, impart a sense of longevity. I added a touch of whimsy to the scene with two bird figurines perched in the window.
Photographs by Patricia McLean

Robert Brown Interior Design, page 190

Todd Richesin Interiors, page 108

Brian Watford Interiors, page 118

Judy Bentley Interior Views, page 154

Patricia McLean Interiors, Inc.

A well-traveled designer, Patricia McLean often reflects her broad view of the world, incorporating antique elements within the framework of classical design. Her knowledge of the basic tenets of design—scale, proportion, color, and balance—as well as her confidence and ease with her craft allow her to impart a sense of *sprezzatura*, or a certain nonchalance. Those who follow her work know that her real talent lies in making rooms feel as if they were decorated over time.

Above: To bring out the family's classic sensibility and taste, I used light fabrics to soften and complement the preferred blue tone on the walls. In the living room, the homeowners' gorgeous French trumeau mirror is highlighted by brackets from the Ann Getty Collection sporting a shell motif that hints at their love of St. Croix and the Caribbean. Handpainted Chinese panels in gilt frames, silk draperies, plaid club chairs, and a coir rug provide a wonderful juxtaposition between old and new.

Facing Page: Details always make a room. In a nod to European glamour, I combined gilded French *cantonnières* with a brilliant silk drapery fabric with a strié contrast. The divine handpainted wallpaper picks up the tones from every element in the room for a cohesive, collected feel. To encourage conversation, I chose a round, Regency-style antique reproduction table. The antique French chandelier completes the space.
Photographs by Lauren Rubenstein

"Decorating is both a fine art and a science. You need to have an eye for beauty and a knowledge of geometry and spatial orientation." *Patricia McLean*

Above & Right: After a fire at the Georgia Governor's Mansion damaged the ballroom, I was asked by the Governor and First Lady to help create a new look. To play off the marble floors and coordinate with the silk draperies I designed, I commissioned a faux artist for the strié finish in neutral colors. The hand-carved, custom designed wooden drapery pelmet was inspired by the antique Federal mirror, adding another air of regality along with the antique silver from the USS Georgia.
Photographs by Jake Laughlin

Facing Page: The entire family room design started with an antique mirror that I found and showed to the architect, who used it as his inspiration during the project. To enhance the paneling and open up the room, I painted the ceiling a light blue-green and used complementary teal colors in the rug and draperies. The Chippendale cabinet provides a perfect spot for the projector, which utilizes a movie screen that drops from the ceiling in front of the mirror. With children and two dogs, the family needs sturdy materials, so the upholstery is covered in commercial-grade chenille and leather.
Photographs by Lauren Rubenstein

"Selecting the perfect fabric and trim creates fine details that can make a huge impact."
Patricia McLean

Above Left: Accenting a soft wall with bold, antique pieces brings special attention to an area that otherwise might be overlooked. The sunburst mirror is a perfect punctuation atop the gilded framed painting. For balance, I flanked the artwork with two sconces that add light and beauty, function and form.
Photograph by Erica George Dines

Above Right, Facing Page & Previous Pages: A master bedroom at the St. Regis Residences in Atlanta provided a welcome challenge during the 2009 Atlanta Symphony Associates Decorators' Show House. The blank space was large—30 feet by 22 feet—so I created numerous individual vignettes to mimic a Parisian apartment. A substantial table offers an informal eating area in between the elegant bed and the comfortable sitting area, each grounded by their own leopard-print wool rugs. The moulding—which I added as commissioned by an architect—stands out against my own custom color celadon-hued walls. Antique pieces, including the French desk and English chandeliers, collaborate nicely with more contemporary elements.
Above right & previous pages photographs by Lauren Rubenstein
Facing page photograph by Jake Laughlin

Above: The ingenious floorplan of the petite guest house incorporates all of the essentials on the homeowner's wish list, including space for sleeping seven people—which I accomplished through sofa and club chairs that convert into beds. A mirror from India is flanked by Chinese export porcelain and oil paintings that I bought at a Paris flea market. Wide-plank hardwood floors are stained a rich color similar to those found in the Caribbean, and bamboo blinds continue the tropical feel.

Right: For a more relaxed family room, window treatments of yellow hand-blocked linen complement the blue walls. The floral print speaks to the lovely gardens just outside. A sturdy reproduction rug and well-built coffee table provide beauty and the ability to withstand the family's two puppies.

Facing Page: With French doors opening onto the front garden, the gray-green hue was a natural choice that lends an air of seriousness yet remains soft. I commissioned an artist to paint a *faux bois* application on the bookcase to transform the woodwork from stark white to a rich tone for warmth. I continued the masculine feel with a mahogany floor lamp and ladder.
Photographs by Lauren Rubenstein

"Scale is the single most important design element." *Patricia McLean*

Above & Facing Page: A large master bedroom with a beautiful tray ceiling lent inspiration for a Venetian retreat with its existing silk wallpaper, painted ceiling, and antiqued woodwork. A beautiful antique architectural element was fitted as a headboard and really makes a statement in the room. I combined beautiful art and antiques with inviting upholstery and fine fabrics for an elegant yet fresh design. The showpiece of the room is an antique Japanned cabinet produced in 1720 that lived its previous life in an Italian villa. A restriction on adhering anything on the wall led to the solution of ribbons to hide chains that held the artwork. In the sitting area, the illustrious curves of the Venetian *canapé* are carried over to the scalloped edge of the silk drapery and the quatrefoil of the gracious custom ottoman. The hand painted silk panels complement the scheme as well as the gardens outside.
Above photograph by Erica George Dines
Facing page top photograph by Lauren Rubenstein
Facing page bottom photograph by Patricia McLean

Hawkins Israel

As the granddaughter of Harry Hayden Hawkins, who established Hawkins Israel in 1929, Jane has an innate passion for design. In Jane's three-decade career, she has designed many home interiors and developed even more friendships. Although she enjoys creating vacation homes in the mountains and at the beach, her first love is designing the places that people call home, beautiful primary residences throughout the city.

Above: James Carter, a noted Birmingham architect and close personal friend, designed my home. The living room is one of my favorite rooms because of its perfect proportion and balance. Blended with the right colors and beautiful furnishings and décor, the room is comfortable and inviting.

Facing Page: Small yet intimate, the dining room has a charming ambience.
Photographs by Colleen Duffley

"The most wonderful antiques show up when you least expect them." *Jane Hawkins Hoke*

Above & Facing Page: Framed antique greige wallpaper panels are the focal point of the living room. They reiterate the space's beautiful size and scale and complement the neutral palette.

Right: The home has great architectural bones, and the interior design's rustic quality furthers the aesthetic. I always look to the architecture when I'm establishing the tone of an interior because it's the most prominent part of any design.
Photographs by Lee Puckett

Above: The coromandel screen is a perfect complement to the ebony grand piano on the opposite wall of the living room. The black touches lend strength to the soft cream palette.
Photograph by Sylvia Martin

Right & Facing Page Bottom: Bookcases work in almost any room and serve as both functional elements and architectural details. Cookbooks in the cozy breakfast room are charming, and leather-bound books are right at home in the formal dining room, elegantly paired with Italian marble busts.
Right photograph by Sylvia Martin
Facing page bottom photograph by Lee Puckett

Facing Page Top: Revisiting the classics is a wonderful exercise, and I did just that in order to design the bed. It is inspired by the past and sized, detailed, and finished to fit the character of the room, its romantic teal floral fabric, and the garden views.
Photograph by Lee Puckett

Previous Pages: A fabulous Italian villa hidden in the heart of Birmingham has one of the most exquisite private collections of antiques and art that I have had the pleasure of helping to acquire. Collecting beautiful antiques over the years gives a room a sense of time; the living room is warm and charming because it is filled with antiques that the owner has loved for many years.
Photograph by Lee Puckett

Above & Right: The living room flows to the outdoors on the loggia, continuing the earth-tone palette.

Facing Page: The Italian screen is painted in such wonderfully earthy colors—terracotta red, teal blue, and buttery cream—that it inspired the color palette for the entire first floor.
Photographs by Colleen Duffley

Alcott Interiors

Carolyn Kendall, owner of Alcott Interiors, designs homes to reflect the homeowners' lifestyles and personalities. Through close collaboration with the homeowners, Carolyn makes sure each room functions well and simultaneously combines beautiful furnishings and objects from different time periods and origins to make the home unique and interesting. Passionate about finding just the right piece to set off a space, the design team is constantly expanding its views and sources. Whether it is a transitionally furnished casual home or a historically based Georgian residence filled with antiques, the results are consistent in their classic elegance and attention to detail.

Above & Facing Page: The transitional family room was designed as a comfortable and peaceful retreat for a very active family of five. The reclaimed wood floors and beams and rough stone fireplace create a backdrop for the warm color palette, textural fabrics, and comfortable furnishings we selected. Details such as the European iron fragments that were turned into light fixtures on the mantel emanate an aged character and a nice glow in the evenings. For further interest and a more intimate feel, we added beautifully printed linen draperies, a custom chandelier, and furniture with modern lines.
Photographs by Bob Shatz

Above: The light-filled morning room captures a warm, cheery feel perfect for sipping coffee as the sun rises. The custom mosaic floor pattern is mirrored in pattern and color by a stained glass ceiling. We used the silk embroidered draperies and antique chest and daybed to give an aged elegance and softness to a very elegant room.

Facing Page: The new Belle Meade home's living room features all of the benefits of a new home while also embracing the aged character of a historical Georgian residence. A gilded bronze French chandelier, an antique lyre-based table, and a heavily inlaid tea table are all unique pieces that help to define the quality and European influence that was important to us in creating a historical interior. We collaborated with Eric Stengel Architecture to create flow and cohesiveness from the outside in.
Photographs by Bob Shatz

"Design at its best is a perfect balance of beauty and function." *Carolyn Kendall*

"One of the most enjoyable aspects of design is the good friends you make along the way."
Carolyn Kendall

Above: Scalamandré gold linen pheasant fabric was my starting point for the paneled library, where rich brown hues contrast with gold, green, and red to impart life and interest. A lovely antique table desk along with a pair of comfortable shield back chairs and a leopard print tufted ottoman allow the room to be used as a study as well as a cozy place for the parents of four to put up their feet.
Photograph by Howard E. Kelley

Facing Page: I love to use antique pieces to personalize spaces and give them interest and aged elegance. One of my favorite finds is the enormous French chandelier in the two-story stairwell that adds sparkle and beauty. The mixed-metal handrail and stained glass skylight help create a one-of-a-kind space. We worked with Eric Stengel Architecture to make a historically based home that is very comfortable in today's world.
Photograph by Bob Shatz

Above: The master bathroom design began with an intricate stone mosaic border that the homeowner fell in love with. The neutral stone complements the border, while a terracotta marble countertop brings out more vibrancy and life. We created a recessed area for the free-standing tub, complete with vinyl damask wallpaper and marble shelves for a private oasis. The antique sconces and chandelier, along with the silk valance and privacy-enhancing café panels, add interest to the bathroom.
Photographs by Bob Shatz

Facing Page Top: Used primarily to entertain, the comfortable yet elegant living room of a 1920s Georgian home perfectly reflects the family. The bergère chairs and ottoman are a favorite resting place when a warm fire is going. French antiques and the luxurious fabric and draperies give the room a formal feel; by pairing them with a sisal rug, we reduced the formality just a bit to make it comfortable for all.
Photograph by Howard E. Kelley

Facing Page Bottom: The serene master bedroom color palette of soft blues, bright greens, and golds contrasts against rich stained wood and a gilded chandelier to embody a welcoming and unique feel. I used a beautiful antique linen press with French polish finish and oval-shaped doors to conceal the television.
Photograph by Howard E. Kelley

Annelle Primos & Associates

Beautiful antiques, comfortable fabrics, and classic style are the building blocks for Annelle Primos. Understanding the importance of an interior that can grow with those residing in it, Annelle tends to avoid trendy items and instead builds a room with neutral furnishings that beckons the homeowner to enjoy the space. She then weaves in a few contemporary pieces and a bit of color for a striking appearance. Every project is uniquely created for the homeowner's preferences and lifestyle—which Annelle is quite adept at discerning. Then she uses her art background and its ideas about color, shape, and spatial relationship to refine the concepts and reflect the residents.

Above & Facing Page: A quiet but strong painting by French artist Pierre Brisson sets the mood for the entire home. I integrated a few contemporary pieces into a warm mix of eclectic finds: porcupine quill box, African sculpture, framed Kuba cloth, Ethiopian shields, and African-inspired textiles. The homeowners' love of entertaining dictated a plethora of seating options, like benches and leather folding chairs that can be moved from room to room. Flanking the fireplace, built-in bookshelves express the residents' love of reading and appropriately display collected items. Of utmost importance was durability and comfort; two young sons, a dog, and adults with red wine are free to enjoy the natural chenille sofa and leather chairs.
Photographs by Charlie Godbold

Above & Right: Interiors shouldn't be perfect; they need a few contrasting elements to keep the space interesting. In a traditional dining room, I used a contemporary painting by Carol Sneed and a modern sculpture juxtaposed with the soft Swedish clock, green silk curtains, antique French chairs, and Italian chandelier. In a bedroom, the simple, 18th-century Swedish chest embraces its sculptural lines when paired with a gilded ornate mirror.

Facing Page: Downsizing into a smaller home prompted the homeowner to keep only the things she truly treasured—mainly artwork and sculptural Tang dynasty horses that I incorporated throughout the residence. In contrast to her former home, a lighter look was achieved with pieces such as the contemporary shagreen chest and the soft velvet pillows.
Photographs by Charlie Godbold

"You must own the house; it shouldn't own you." *Annelle Primos*

Above: Even with neutral fabrics, the entire bedroom speaks of rich traditions and a sense of comfort and luxury, derived from the use of sumptuous linens and furnishings that the homeowner already owned: a sofa from her grandmother and a chair that was one of her first fine purchases nearly 30 years ago.

Facing Page Top: A light ambience suggests quietness and allows the beautiful art to become the center of attention. I utilized a combination of antiques and reproduction pieces that achieve soft, subtle details.

Facing Page Bottom: A husband and wife needed a room that offered a calm, comfortable atmosphere to come home to after their frequent travels. Using pale platinum and soft blush tones, a silk velvet sofa, and a plush rug, I gave them an oasis with both contemporary and antique pieces interspersed throughout.
Photographs by Charlie Godbold

J. Edwards Interiors

Designers are, in effect, part visionaries and part realists. They must see the ideas that the homeowner may describe—or create a vision based on their own observations of the homeowner's lifestyle—and then be able to translate that ideal dream into a realistic plan without losing the original excitement or goal. For Jenny Edwards, this delicate balance between the vision and practical execution is second nature. From growing up in an artistic, well-designed environment where everyone respected what they had, Jenny has held onto her roots and developed a talent for seeing fresh ideas and knowing how to use them to design tasteful, beautiful spaces.

Above: The entire living room evolved from the colors in the Mexican tile fireplace. I enforced a neutral tone on most of the large elements to impart an inviting ambience, then interjected a few blue and orange hues to give life to the space. The blue ceramic pedestal table and the colorful painting really tie everything in with the fireplace. Layering the Oushak rugs on top of a seagrass floor covering visually separates the multiple seating areas while maintaining unity throughout the large room.

Facing Page: My favorite style is eclectic; I love to mix antique pieces with more modern elements. In a corner that just seemed a bit bare, I added a vintage French chest of drawers with a funky piece of art. The chair embraces the lines of an antique French chair, but adds a modern element with its Lucite material. The space is softened with the beautiful printed linen drapery and the antique Oushak rug.
Photographs by Beau Gustafson

Above: The master bedroom in a transitional home reflects the young, hip couple but still feels like a calming, inviting retreat away from their three children. I designed the space with neutral tones and a few pops of muted color interspersed with modern accessories, such as the alabaster lamp. Individual nightstands are functional and complement his and her sides of the bed. An architect table in the back nook allows a quiet place for studying and reading.

Facing Page Top Left & Bottom: Mixing styles can be a challenge, but the technique is actually an easy way to update a room quickly without having to buy everything new. I like to add modern lamps, contemporary art, and a few accessories to antique furnishings to give the room an entirely new look. Even reupholstering a traditional chair in a more modern fabric can give the piece an updated look. Use a common thread throughout the design—such as a color or shape—to help the space feel intentional.

Facing Page Top Right: Bright lantern sconces, a ceramic mosaic tile floor, and dual cabinets present the perfect bathroom for a little boy. It is playful yet will still be appropriate as he grows.
Photographs by Beau Gustafson

"A good designer will step out of her comfort zone." *Jenny Edwards*

"A few expensive pieces can give the illusion that the rest of the room is of the same category, too." *Jenny Edwards*

Above & Right: The living room incorporates a touch of concrete at the fireplace, linking the space to the foyer where a solid wall of concrete runs the length of the hallway to create a bench and form one side of the concrete stairway. The Italian lines of the sofa and the smooth leather on the hallway bench provide a few curves amidst the clean lines.

Facing Page: The architect of a very modern home used a lot of natural materials and let those materials speak for themselves. I did not want to cover up the gorgeous bones of the home, so the furnishings and accessories were kept to a minimum. The lighting became a large focus; it presented a welcome opportunity to add in a few playful elements with the funky sconce that threw rays onto the wall and the custom chandelier over the dining table. The mix of materials, especially the glass doors that separate the dining area from the kitchen, soften the hard edges of the wood.
Photographs by Beau Gustafson

J. Hirsch Interior Design

Not just a blank canvas in which to design, a home is a collection of architectural elements to enhance and adjust, according to Janie Hirsch, ASID. First captivated by her father's architectural career and then expanded through her own formal education, an appreciation for architectural elements has given her a unique lens through which she views a home. Starting with quality furnishings, Janie captures the essence of the architectural design through color, fabric, and accessories and blends in the homeowner's personality and lifestyle. In the end, each space exudes a smart ambience that will age gracefully.

Above & Facing Page: Inspired by the homeowner's love of Scandinavia, I generated a Swedish feel for the dining room and adjoining music area through neutral tones and clean lines. Pine floors with a grey wash and light finishes on the furniture exude a handsome contrast with the dark charcoal walls; a pop of color with paprika pillows cheers the space up. Natural materials—a linen curtain and dining chairs, wool armchairs, and silk pillows—maintain the regional atmosphere. The design—which also lends itself to a gallery feel—showcases the homeowner's appreciation for art.
Photographs by Chris Little Photography

Above & Left: In keeping with the Scandinavian ambience of the home, I brought in muted colors for the living room and master bedroom. Lighter tones of pale yellow and blue-grey on the walls emanate a relaxing feel, despite the home's urban location. Soft accents in both rooms contribute to an elegant, but not feminine, space. A custom headboard—created from chunky picture frame moulding—establishes a focal point; chandeliers in place of traditional lamps in the bedroom and the charcoal lampshade in the living room offer dramatic punch.

Facing Page: Auburn University built a new student village with buildings designed for Greek society use. The main floor in each building houses a number of different chapter rooms, and I was thrilled to design my sorority's common areas. Classic lines and a slate blue and brown color palette generate a long-lasting style and chic sophistication, very appropriate for young ladies. Because the space needed to function in many capacities—for studying, social gatherings, watching TV, and relaxing—I incorporated multiple areas. Sconces and lamps bring the lighting closer to eye level for a more intimate space.
Photographs by Chris Little Photography

"Natural fibers are excellent for any design because they breathe and generate an inherent lightness." *Janie Hirsch*

"Consider highlighting one of the most expansive areas in a room—the floor—with a quality rug, hardwood laid in a unique pattern, or with paint." *Janie Hirsch*

Above & Facing Page: While not every exterior commands the design of the interior, the façade of a suburban Atlanta residence certainly meshed with the desires of the homeowners. I took cues from the European exterior to transform the home into an Italian farmhouse. Handcrafted, reclaimed wood floors and ripped pine beams provide the Old World structure. Throughout the design, elements were added to make it appear as if the home had been designed over the years and that everything had been passed down through the generations. A plaster-like appearance on select walls, a European approach to color—through the use of both warm and cool tones—and a mismatched but blended collection of antique and contemporary furniture and accessories give off a handsome feel.
Photographs by Chris Little Photography

Sarah Jones Interiors

From a young age, Sarah Nelson, Allied Member ASID, was passionate about beautiful environments. In fact, she would often arrange freshly picked flowers to brighten up her home, much to her mother's surprise. As a child, she didn't comprehend the reason behind that zeal, but maturity brought the understanding that pleasant surroundings can dramatically affect a person's outlook. Whether she's working on an urban residence for a young couple, a penthouse for a refined bachelor, or a sprawling country manor for a multi-generational family, Sarah, along with her associate Catherine Graeber, create designs that resonate with Sarah's goal to improve the surroundings by adding value to everyday life.

Above & Facing Page: Built in the 1930s as the Elks Lodge, the downtown Jackson building was restored by architect Alfred Luckett as an art gallery on the first floor and the owner's residence on the third floor. We maintained as much of the original building as possible—including the heart pine floors and windows—and then designed the residence as an extension of the gallery. Sleek, urban elements, such as the exposed ductwork, stainless steel appliances, and art hung from wire, speak of the gallery ambience. At the same time, the home generates a refined, elegant feel with warm colors, comfortable seating and bedding, and grand moulding.
Photographs by Hubert Worley

"A beautiful home must include some degree of organization." *Sarah Nelson*

Above, Right & Facing Page: While raising three children, a young couple decided to move out of the metropolitan atmosphere and into Oxford, which is home to the University of Mississippi and is also considered one of the best places to retire. Their new home reflected a French country look, with architectural designs by Frank Tindall. Exposed natural materials—such as the brick arch between the living and dining areas, rough-hewn beams on the living room ceiling, and natural plank ceiling in the den—lend themselves to the rural European ambience. We punctuated the spaces with soft, warm fabrics to impart serenity, which emulates the swimming pool and large park just behind the home. With many seating areas and cozy rooms interspersed throughout, every family member has a space to relax.
Photographs by Hubert Worley

Above, Left & Facing Page: Whether we're working in the city or in a rural area, our first priority is to delve into the homeowners' lives and understand what makes them tick. During a renovation for a 20-year-old penthouse, the couple expressed a desire to design with an elegant, contemporary vibe. In every room in the home, we embraced clean lines, sleek elements, and muted colors with a few bright hues interjected. A handful of antique elements ground the home, while modern artwork adds a bit of flair. Minimal accessories allow those chosen to stand out, and the use of multiple mirrors and shiny elements generates an upscale feeling with a contemporary vibe.
Photographs by Greg Campbell

"The more drastically different each of my projects, the more interesting they become."
Sarah Nelson

Todd Richesin Interiors

Todd Richesin thrives on the chance to enhance people's unique color preferences by introducing interesting patterns and textures. He is not afraid of working with color or having fun with it. In metropolitan settings, where outside views are often lacking, he makes the most of interior spaces by using color and texture in unexpected ways. Todd's interiors display his mastery of color, insistence on detail, fondness for gorgeous fabrics, and ability to find the true heart of a home—regardless of size. His work is all about comfort and Southern charm.

Above: The dining room brilliantly meets extended family entertainment needs. A large rectangular table seats 10, two small tables accommodate eight more, and the sunroom on the other side of the kitchen seats everybody else—without having to bring in extra chairs. The owners asked for an elegant, sophisticated look to complement the Williamsburg-style house. While the Colonial Williamsburg blue honors the historic context, the décor gives the room a more finished look.
Photograph by Larsen Jay, DoubleJay Creative

Facing Page: The foyer of my own home was architecturally uninteresting, so I added the paneling to heighten the style. The 18th-century commode and 19th-century Dutch painting lend a regal quality to the entryway. The painting's color scheme inspired the palette of the entire home, the epitome of Southern elegance.
Photograph by Werner Straub

Above: I renovated my home to embody classical French Norman style. Because it is filled with 18th- and 19th-century Continental treasures—both antiques and artwork—it has a distinct sense of history, despite the modern amenities that have become such an important facet of daily life. Each time you wander through a space, your eye picks up something different, which keeps the home visually interesting and stimulating. Ceiling treatments, wall finishes, furnishings, mouldings, textiles, and every other fixed and movable part of the home are in keeping with the desired historic tradition.

Facing Page Top: The den is grounded by a circa-1890 Oushak. While the fabulous chest from Provence conceals much of the audiovisual technology, I decided to keep the television in full display because when it's on there's no point in hiding it and when it's off all you notice are the beautiful paintings next to it anyhow.

Facing Page Bottom: We acquired the rouge royal marble mantelpiece in Paris a few years before we even owned the house, and upon realizing what a perfect fit it was—both physically and stylistically—we were absolutely ecstatic. Above the mantel hangs the first piece of fine art we ever acquired, which is dear to our hearts and really got us hooked on fine-quality antique pieces. The adjacent foyer is graced with a chandelier from a mansion in Atlanta and a Kirman rug made in honor of a loved one; it's signed by the maker.
Photographs by Werner Straub

"Great designs are rooted in authenticity, so start with what you love and build from there."
Todd Richesin

Above Left: Designing for well-traveled individuals is a particular treat because of the opportunity to showcase wonderful finds from all over the world—it's instant authentic inspiration. The sunroom, with its slate fireplace wall and side walls clad in tree bark sourced from North Carolina, features a few such travel mementos.

Above Right & Facing Page Top: The adjoining breakfast room and kitchen have an easy elegance about them. A bit of their majolica is displayed along the back wall, and cookbooks are artistically displayed and readily accessible. As elsewhere in the home, these spaces have simple iron light fixtures, which are functional and beautiful, but not too showy. The lack of upper cabinetry is both a modernist statement and a response to the petite cook's needs.

Facing Page Bottom: The sunlit room is designed around the fabulous headboard, an old door from Thailand. The hand-painted nightstands from Italy and the soft linen coverlet fabric by Bennison really bring the whole room together.
Photographs by Werner Straub

Amy D. Morris Interiors

People want choices, but they also appreciate the solid recommendation of someone who knows them, understands their lifestyle, and has a great idea of what will bring them joy. Enter Amy Morris, a designer who has not only a great aesthetic sense but also a knack for reading people and knowing what their spaces need. She is inspired by each home's residents as well as its locale: Waterfront vacation properties just beg for a light and airy design while single-family residences in the city or suburbs offer the chance to create warm, tranquil settings.

Above: Many people don't realize how much you can do with spaces that have decorative paneling, so they either resort to a safe design of symmetrically hung paintings or simply leave the walls blank. But when you can create an interesting composition that's balanced, it merges the architectural and interior design into a really pleasing look.

Facing Page: When choosing textiles, I tend to go with wearable fabrics like cotton, linen, and velvet that feel nice on your skin. In the living room, the damask draperies offer just a touch of pattern, while various tones of taupe furniture and accessories add depth. The mirror has the character of an antique, which is the perfect complement to the collection of vintage botanical prints.
Photographs by Emily Followill

Above & Left: The reclaimed beams inspired a casual, elegant look in the adjacent kitchen and family room spaces. Because there's such a variety in the furniture stains, the rooms feel collected rather than forced. Although it's sort of unusual, the kitchen design doesn't include upper cabinets on the back wall. Instead, the window has room to breathe and the wall is tiled from counter to ceiling with crisp white, beveled-edge tiles that really accentuate the rusticity of the beams.

Facing Page: Inspiration for a room can start with just about anything: a priceless antique needlepoint sofa and Oushak rug, a couple's preference of soft neutrals and symmetry, or a unique canopy bed. I'm really drawn to the look of juxtaposed elements—old and new, light and dark, smooth and textural.
Photographs by Emily Followill

"It's about simplifying and choosing pieces that you really love." *Amy Morris*

Brian Watford Interiors

The ability to envision the end result is intrinsic in any artist, whether the medium is paint, music, or clay. The same is true for Brian Watford, Allied Member ASID, who has mastered the art of bringing his design visions to life. Because of the personal nature of a home, though, Brian does not create his plan for the space without tremendous input and coordination from each homeowner. After studying the homeowner's lifestyle and soaking in the architectural surroundings, Brian delivers interiors through a process of exposure, education, and creativity, ultimately refining the homeowner's style into something unique that speaks of quality and of the owner's personality.

Above & Facing Page: Although the architecture may often be established long before the interiors are even in the planning stages, the two must be respectful of one another. While the decor doesn't need to exactly mirror the architecture, they should have some connection to help ease the transition. In a home with a Craftsman exterior where the young family appreciated the simplicity of modern design, I incorporated a Mid-Century Modern look indoors to take advantage of the clean lines in both styles. Caned-back chairs and an antiqued round mirror that give an aged appearance along with authentically vintage pieces, like the daybed and Art Deco French sideboard, mix well with the newer furnishings. A collection of styles and a variety of finishes are both essential to achieving a key goal of good design: to generate interest.
Photographs by Deborah Whitlaw Llewellyn

Above: With the homeowner's desire to have a pool house that was classic with modern elements, I worked with the architect to create a structure that is reminiscent of an old European villa, finished in shades of brown and white. Plaster walls with rounded corners, reclaimed wood beams, an iron chandelier, and a concrete coffee table carefully balance a modern aesthetic with an aged feel. Custom upholstery all covered in outdoor fabric makes the room completely usable with no need to worry about water from the pool.
Photograph by Chris Simmons

Facing Page Top: Fabric can play such an integral role. In an enormous master bedroom, I upholstered the walls in a charcoal grey flannel, which softened the noise level and made the room more intimate and restful. The nightstand drawers and headboard were covered with suede and the charcoal grey shagreen bed frame is trimmed with bone. Heavy wool embroidered drapery continues the intimate ambience while a few pops of turquoise and light fabric on smaller elements—like the chair in the sitting room—interject interest and a peaceful aura.
Photographs by Deborah Whitlaw Llewellyn

Facing Page Bottom: The mild climate of the Southeast allows beautiful greenery and flowers to grow, even amidst the metropolitan city. To enhance these surroundings, I designed custom window coverings that, instead of obstructing the views, actually draw the eye outward.
Photograph by Deborah Whitlaw Llewellyn

"Good design is a process that should be unique to each project—an informed, understated collection of past and present...classic with modern sensibility." *Brian Watford*

Brinson Interiors

While a home's design is certainly in tune with its surroundings, Brinson Interiors focuses first and foremost on how the home and its spaces will be used. By injecting a cohesive, underlying theme throughout each project, Wayne Brinson Holder, ASID, melds the need for unpredictability and lively color with the current trend of restful, calm homes. Whether by accentuating a home's architectural details or adding them through wallpaper, pilasters, or similar techniques, each space does not mimic other designs but instead speaks of its own character and style.

Above: Not intimidated by sophisticated furnishings, the homeowner preferred a formal French style. The mantel, from an old Rothschild chateau in France, and the French gilt and crystal cave à liqueur establish the tone for the home. We built a collection of accessories and 18th- and 19th-century European paintings to fit into the environment, maintaining a quiet palette of fabric and wall colors to allow the art and accessories to stand out.

Facing Page: A few well-placed elements can create a beautiful space, so we kept the foyer simple and elegant to capture a classical, serene ambience. A sophisticated marble pattern on the floor allows guests to decompress upon entering, and the antique settee offers a resting place. Along the staircase, the homeowner's art collection follows the curves up to the second floor.
Photographs by Miller Mobley

"Design is about as predictable as the weather." *Wayne Holder*

Above Left: A soothing, tone-on-tone color palette makes the most of the sitting area's abundant natural light. A reproduction French chair, simple silk velvet sofa, and reproduction French guéridon table offer a refined living area.

Above Right & Facing Page: A daughter inherited her mother's very traditional house that was filled with antiques and gave off a somewhat Palm Beach style. However, she preferred something a bit more contemporary, so we transformed the dwelling into a stylish, elegant, comfortable home. Every room was painted a crisp white; the living and dining room feature casual linen drapes with woven shades, laid-back rugs, linen slip-covered furniture, and a coffee table that doubles as a footrest, all designed to establish a simple ambience. We reconfigured the master bedroom and bath to take advantage of the views, adding a touch of soft color with the turquoise silk draperies that feature large dragonflies. The ample space gave us room to include a sofa, numerous chairs, and a reading table.
Photographs by Miller Mobley

Chamberlain Interiors

June Chamberlain, Allied Member ASID, says her designs hinge on relationships—with the space and how it speaks to her, and, most importantly, with the homeowner to determine his or her needs. June then intermingles affordable and investment pieces, which she likens to a person wearing Gap jeans and a Gucci shirt; every item doesn't need to be expensive for an ensemble to work. June's background—antique-collecting parents, an interior design degree, an internship with renowned architect Frank McCall, and a fondness for the Paris flea market—and smart design sense allow her rooms to appear as if their elements were collected over the years.

Above Left & Facing Page: Sometimes a room needs a little warmth, a lived-in feeling. I often will interject a rich color like paprika onto the wall or add an antique Persian rug to the floor to achieve the warm ambience. I can always appreciate a few imperfections, as with an older rug with a few tears or a weathered leather chair covering. Those little bumps along the way reveal a history and bring a sense of character to the space.

Above Right: In homes where square footage is at a minimum, I utilize design techniques to visually add more space. In a condominium, airy fabric allows extra light into the room and a buttery-yellow wall color reflects the sun's rays. I also pare down on accessories and furnishings to allow the room to breathe.
Photographs by Chris Little Photography

"Design is a two-way street—a give-and-take process between the designer and the homeowner—that ends with a beautiful expression of personality in the home."
June Chamberlain

Above & Right: The functionality of a room's design is just as important as the aesthetic aspects of a space. To initiate a soothing atmosphere in a master bedroom, I embraced a cool color palette and lightweight materials—linen draperies and layered, thin quilts. The Italian nightstand and antique architectural element above the bed establish focal points. In the dining room of a family who frequently entertains, I expanded the traditional seating to include antique benches and beautiful high-backed chairs.

Facing Page: Symmetry and scale give a sense of order and balance to large spaces. An appropriately sized piece of contemporary artwork in the large hallway contrasts nicely with the antique desk and chair below. In the generously sized living room, the many sets of pairs generate intimacy and allow every element to feel as if it is rightfully in its own place.
Photographs by Chris Little Photography

Cindy Meador Interiors

Raised to be fearless and a go-getter, Cindy Meador translated those qualities first into a career in fashion and design—in Dallas, New York, and Los Angeles—and then to follow her dream in interior design. Inspired by her mother and grandmother who had exceptional taste and beautiful homes, Cindy has developed an eye for refined, comfortable furnishings and art that are polished and offer a glimpse of glamour. Cindy is never afraid to try something new or offer an out-of-the-ordinary suggestion to a homeowner, and her designs mirror her energetic personality—they are at once cutting edge and timeless.

Above Left: An eclectic combination of many different styles shows that there are virtually no rules. I love the antique French chairs, classic modern mirrored console, Mid-Century metal starbursts, and contemporary art, which embraces a dramatic feeling that is not intimidating.

Above Right & Facing Page: A penthouse on the Alabama coast called for a modern aesthetic that was still soft, inviting, and a little glamorous with just a touch of the coastal feel. The homeowner wanted to stay away from the hard contemporary look. In both the master bedroom and living area, I chose grey-toned walls with splashes of gold to merge with the neutral bedding and comfortable swivel rockers.
Photographs by Parish Stapleton

Above: In contrast to the home's comfortable den, the formal living area is more classic and clean, featuring bergère chairs and a French-inspired fireplace. I grounded the frosty colors with walnut flooring and natural door trim to create a rich feeling throughout the house.

Right: Sentimental items, collections, or personal favorites allow a house to be decorated around the personalities that will reside within its walls. In a Fairhope project, a seashell chandelier spoke to the homeowner so it became the center of attention in the decidedly eclectic breakfast area.

Facing Page: I designed the Alabama penthouse dining area to exude Hollywood glamour. With a classic table and rug, the French candlestick lamps add a hint of an antique feeling to the luxurious chairs, rich drapery, and stunning light fixture.
Photographs by Parish Stapleton

Circa Interiors & Antiques

Creating a timeless design requires a keen eye and a deep understanding of past trends. For Cindy Smith, founder of Circa Interiors, those attributes translate into a refined ability to extract just the right elements from certain periods to create a classic, functional ambience that can be enjoyed for years to come. Her foundation for each room centers on quality furniture that won't tire over time. Mixed with her proclivity to combine well-established pieces with new ones, conventional with contemporary, the quality furnishings impart a quiet but confident style.

Above: Relaxed surroundings and an exceptional view embrace the enduring essence of the juxtaposed ancient and contemporary elements. I placed classic pewter, weathered books, and an 18th-century Belgian tapestry on the desk next to the clean lines of the high-backed chair and refined drapery.
Photograph by Pat Staub Photography

Facing Page: Modern furnishings don't always equate to metallic finishes or outlandish colors. In a traditional home, the smooth silhouette of the fabric-encased chairs appropriately contrasts the classic table and formal chandelier. For continuity, I maintained a tone-on-tone color palette, with the exception of the lavender and bright green table accents.
Photograph by Steven Young Photography

Above: My goal for the outdoor area was to express a lifestyle approach to entertaining so that everyday occurrences could easily morph into a party. The altar bench was taken out of its natural placement on the floor and set on the Belgian slate tabletop to provide the perfect pedestal for candles. At night, the setting turns into a breathtaking scene. During the day, the subtle connection between the touch of lavender on the table and the surrounding lamb's ear and sage creates a charming atmosphere.
Photograph by Steven Young Photography

Facing Page Top Left: I like to bring in one piece that really impacts a room; something of exceptional quality can forge an enormous difference in the setting, making a room memorable as well as beautiful. The Italian chandelier, pieced together from 17th- and 18th-century fragments, is simple and romantic without being fussy and animates an otherwise commonplace room.
Photograph by Pat Staub Photography

Facing Page Middle Left: The small, unexpected pop of color lends a whimsical flavor to the beautiful, 18th-century reproduction settee. I learned the homeowner loved purple and immediately jumped at the chance to express her personality in the design. I implemented the color in a way that can be easily changed in the future.
Photograph by Steven Young Photography

Facing Page Bottom Left & Right: Fabric transforms a space through texture and color, with details adding personality and style. In a living room, neutral colors embrace a tranquil ambience and a custom nailhead design on the ottoman punctuates a refined style. Foyers can often feel sterile, so a cozy window seat with subtle details on the plump pillows establishes warmth and softness.
Photographs by Steven Young Photography

Design Lines

Judy Pickett, FASID, describes her work as interpretive. When she meets a homeowner, she begins a journey to discover what that person loves and what puts a smile on his or her face. Finding the common thread, she weaves that link throughout a space, bumping the initial vision into the next realm to exceed expectations. The journey includes anticipating the homeowner's aesthetic and functional needs, determining how to reflect those in smart, beautiful rooms, and then helping the homeowner visualize the possibilities. In short, Judy calls herself and her team of designers "lifestyle advocates."

Above: With designer Molly Simmons, ASID, at the helm, we transformed a master bedroom into an elegant retreat perfect for reading a good book. The bay window featuring a lovely view offers the ideal spot for a luxurious chenille chaise. A drum table and ethereal lamp nestle up to the chaise for function and beauty. Silk damask drapery with loop ribbon fringe hugs the window, and hidden reed shades can be closed to block out all light.
Photograph by Sam Gray Photography

Facing Page: An upscale, Tudor-style townhome called for a fresh, approachable design inside. The entire home's scheme centers on a palette of black and white, so we continued the tradition in the dining room with a bone chandelier, a black border painted on the hardwood floor, and a refined black china hutch. The accessories create large bold shapes with an occasional pop of color.
Photograph by Ray Barbour Photography

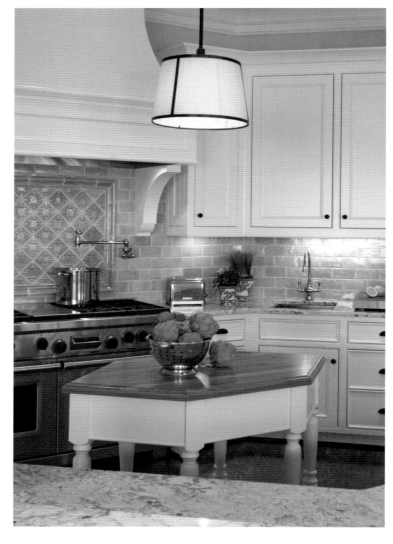

Above: I love to use items that were collected through the years, especially when they come from all over the world. In a family room adjacent to the kitchen, a rug purchased overseas provided the inspiration. Its touch of coral prompted the warm wall color, and the global feel plays out in the accessories and art throughout the room.
Photograph by Sam Gray Photography

Facing Page Top & Bottom Right: Many times a light, airy feel and an open concept are the perfect ambience for a kitchen, especially when family gathers in the space. Depending on the family dynamics, design details are adjusted to provide more functionality, like a custom-designed island to provide an eat-in space or to mimic the shape of the surrounding countertops. Cozy elements, like the shade chandelier, add a familiar quality.
Photographs by Ray Barbour Photography

Facing Page Bottom Left: For a second bedroom, Molly envisioned a modern, multifunctional approach with an Asian flair. Using minimal square footage, a chaise provided a bed for guests as well as a spot to lounge and work on the computer. The dual-purpose space allowed room for a treadmill and bookshelf, yet felt uncluttered and welcoming with its clean lines, textured floor covering, and calming neutral colors.
Photograph by Ray Barbour Photography

"A designer should be the ultimate observer, conscious of how the surroundings make you feel." *Judy Pickett*

Essary & Murphy

Location has everything to do with how people live. It influences their tastes as well as what they do in their spare time. Wherever they design, James Essary and Bill Murphy like to begin projects with people's collections, which speak volumes about their lifestyles and interests. Sometimes just a few pieces need to be showcased; other times, it's a matter of consolidating related items into one special place where, together, they can make a dramatic statement. If the homeowners have no collections to speak of, the founding principals of Essary & Murphy are pros at helping people hone in on meaningful decorative objects.

Above & Facing Page: The homeowners' love of Italian elegance is embedded in their home, from the Palladian-style architecture to the smallest of decorative furnishings. They're a well-traveled couple, whose home reads like a journal of wonderful, global experiences. Chinese pottery and sculpture dating back to the Han Dynasty are showcased above the fireplace, a nod to the earthen material's origins. It holds its own against the impressive collection of 18th-century European dog paintings, hung eclectically against walls that are finished with judges paneling. The monochromatic tone of the draperies, walls, trimwork, and stone mantelpiece serves as a neutral backdrop for the art.
Photographs by Chris Little Photography

Above & Right: Flexible entertaining space is paramount for the philanthropist residents. Easy circulation is created by the gracious rooms, which open to terraces and are connected with wide openings. Painted pilasters and ceiling beams subtly create conversation areas within the large living room. The soft color of all of the surfaces, furnishings, and textiles draws attention to the collection of camel and horse sculptures. Rather than hanging a painting above the fireplace, we chose an antiqued mirror so that nothing distracts from the sacred antique urns. While the room is rooted in classicism with elements like the Regency pedestal table and armchairs, the Lucite and glass coffee table brings the setting into the 21st century—it's the best of historic and modern.

Facing Page: Beautiful 17th- and 18th-century porcelain vessels and plates provide pops of color against the creamy, hand-painted wallpaper. Because a banquette table would have felt too formal, we went with two round tables that seat 12 for dinner or accommodate even more for a standing-room-only hors d'oeuvres party. The Italian inlaid chests and Trumeau-style mirror add to the room's elegance.
Photographs by Chris Little Photography

Jackie Naylor Interiors

Even in the most formal space, Jackie Naylor, ASID, weaves in at least one element that adds flair or spark to enhance the room. In this way she takes what could be mundane and tweaks it just enough to transform the space into something memorable. Inserting her imagination into the materials, texture, and color, Jackie then builds on that extraordinary element and ensures each area resembles the homeowner. With a passion that brings life to the home, Jackie guarantees each room will not only feel like it belongs in the home but will also feel as if the home were built around the room.

Above & Facing Page: Even if a certain color or style is requested by the homeowner, I still have fun playing with the finishes and textures to create a thoughtfully designed space. In an urban condo, a homeowner carried blue tones throughout the residence and enjoyed a modern, refined ambience. I had seen the Zettel'z chandelier, which artfully replaces traditional crystals with stationery, and felt it would add the perfect touch of whimsy and style. The homeowner loved it and now asks guests to write a note and pin it to the chandelier. In her master bedroom, patterned fabrics expand the muted hues and metallic accents punctuate the space. The acrylic waterfall bench almost disappears but ends up capturing the eye.
Photographs by Robert Thien

"A space that has practicality and elegance will sustain itself over time." *Jackie Naylor*

Above & Right: A variety of finishes and materials, although quite diverse, can forge a unique expression. To highlight the homeowner's significant Franco Jonda art collection, I chose clean, modern elements that would subtly animate the spaces. In the living room, a stainless steel fireplace surround, wenge storage cabinets flanking the fireplace, and a mid-century glass coffee table—repurposed from the original décor—embody clean lines yet establish a sophisticated feel. Slightly tufted wool carpet meets hatched-leather floor tile in the hallway, integrating the mesh-backed stainless steel flooring in the kitchen and marble in the kitchen's seating area. Despite the eclectic materials, the design elements blend so well that their differences are hardly noticed.

Facing Page: Occasionally a space can be designed around one element—like a bathtub. Custom molded by the homeowner out of scagliola stone—a blend of marble, travertine, and limestone—the tub is traditional with a slight tweak in style. To continue the established ambience, I embraced a standard, refined tile with a traditional glaze and simple chrome-based vanities. A ghost chair and modern artwork by Jimmy O'Neal—acrylic paint on sanded Plexiglas—spice up the space with metallic finishes and ensure everything is complementary.
Photographs by Robert Thien

Jane Shelton

Designing a room is like working a puzzle; the pieces fit together to accomplish the look. The placement of accessories, the main furnishings, and the lighting blend together to achieve the desired atmosphere. Jane Shelton has been thoughtfully combining numerous elements into warm, functional spaces for so long and so successfully that she has become synonymous with exquisite style. Her designs have been translated into a line of fabrics featured in showrooms throughout the U.S. as well as in London.

Above: An inviting, friendly ambience was a requirement for the family room. I used a variety of fabrics with underlying similarities in color to give a cozy but sophisticated feeling. The classic English carpet grounds the room with its vibrant pattern. A pair of elegant Paris chairs in a Jane Shelton paisley fabric add life to the space.

Facing Page: The entry hall speaks volumes about a home. It should be welcoming yet make a statement. With such intriguing architectural details as a domed ceiling, I wanted to maintain clean lines. Large plants in lattice planters create a natural transition from the lush grounds to the indoors. The custom tables and mirrors set the tone of understated elegance that prevails throughout.
Photographs by James Patterson Photography

Above: Texture and a pop of color in the banquette draw guests into the spacious entry. With its muted, warm tones, the custom wallpaper complements the marble floor. An antique lantern and wall sconces fit well into the beautifully proportioned Georgian space.

Right: Elements of comfort and style in a family breakfast room include birch bark walls, leather chairs, and an antique light fixture.

Facing Page Top: Artwork plays an important role in every room; the homeowner's art is the star of the light-filled living room. A neutral palette combined with splashes of color give freshness to the space. Mixing traditional and more contemporary pieces reflects the sophisticated taste of the homeowner.

Facing Page Bottom Left: Vibrant cantaloupe walls, an antique Oushak rug, and Louis XV leather chairs meld to create drama in the dining room.

Facing Page Bottom Right: Matching club chairs in a stunning green fabric blend with an antique, painted Italian chest and an equestrian painting in a corner of the elegant living room.
Photographs by James Patterson Photography

Judy Bentley Interior Views

In every space designed by Judy Bentley of Interior Views, you're sure to find color and a focal point. Through color, Judy reflects the homeowner's personality and impacts a room in a lot of ways through its hue, reflective qualities, texture, and combination with other colors. In order to ground the room and make a statement, she highlights a specific piece of furniture, a stunning accessory, or even the architectural details. The other elements in the room are hardly forgotten, though. Judy carefully maximizes each aspect of a space, taking full advantage of her innate attention to detail to ensure the design is distinguished and ultimately satisfying.

Above: An Atlanta townhome reflects my penchant for blue and white tones and for entertaining. The collections on the bookshelves really make the table in the great room come alive, while the leopard pillows on the other side of the space add some zip to the otherwise traditional ambience.

Facing Page: The dining room's bay window is the perfect location for the sideboard, which was one of the first antique pieces the homeowner purchased after she got married. The lemonade tone on the walls complements the aqua drapery and the hues in the porcelain lamps. I love the trunk that was from Hong Kong, and, despite its drastically different style, it pairs nicely with the sideboard.
Photographs by Erica George Dines

Above, Right & Facing Page: As a 30th anniversary present to his wife, the husband had their new townhome decorated. As empty nesters, they were experiencing an entirely new concept of living, so I purchased practically everything new. To exude a soothing ambience, vanilla and taupe hues were used throughout the space with just a few red accents interspersed among the rooms. I incorporated a combination of new, antique, and reproduction pieces in the home but knit it all together in a chic, timeless style. A number of metal accents, such as the handles on the chair backs, add a touch of whimsy and an unexpected flourish.
Photographs by Emily Followill

Knight Carr & Company

Just as life involves many different layers, every room is full of layers of elements that evolve the mind and affect the human spirit. Linda Knight Carr's philosophy expresses a conviction that design is more than satisfying spatial needs. It's about the mood of a space and the comfort of individuals who will interact within the room. Each layer provides a glimpse into the life and personality of a home and its residents. The resulting interiors are thoughtful, timeless environments, whether the setting is a beach house, former embassy, yacht, or private jet.

Above: In conjunction with the lifestyle and priorities of the family and their preference for comfortable, Old World style in their new home, I created intimacy in the dining room with a round table for small, seated dinner parties while ample space exists for larger groups to mingle and enjoy hors d'oeuvres and wine from the nearby custom wine cellar. The Persian carpet provided color direction, and its medallion shapes inspired the extraordinary hand-blocked wallpaper, as well as the chair design and its lush damask pattern.
Photograph by Greg Browning

Facing Page: Once an embassy, the city brownstone naturally lends itself to a sophisticated, serious mood with mahogany walls and 15-foot ceilings, but the family enjoys informal entertaining amidst the antiques. I respected the home's history with classically regal elements—French wing chair, carved Italian chest, and ornate sconces. A fresh color scheme was juxtaposed with comfortable seating to reflect an embracing ambience.
Photograph by Gordon Beall

Above & Facing Page Bottom: An early 19th-century Southern farmhouse is a wonderful study in contrasts. The exterior is a typical Greek Revival farmhouse, and the interior boasts elegance through handmade quality craftsmanship, particularly in the plaster mouldings and woodwork. Flanking the foyer, the dining and living rooms present a hospitable atmosphere, executed in a sophisticated manner with shades of blue and forgiving child- and boot-proof fabrics. Based on architectural elements, I used symmetry through proportion as a motif throughout, allowing subtle differences to impart interest.

Facing Page Top: With visions of relaxing after a long day's work, the homeowners requested a comfortably timeless space for conversing with family and friends. The tapestry, mirror, and clock are classic French antiques I acquired through European shopping trips. The closeness of the inviting chairs and the ample circulation around the seating circle embrace a cozy feel.
Photographs by Gordon Beall

Lisa Torbett Interiors

Designing with a renewed sense of tradition lends an established yet fresh air to a space. By incorporating traditional elements in a clean, sophisticated aesthetic—where the homeowners feel comfortable and their lifestyle is embraced—a room can be brought to life in an unexpected way. Relying on their formal education and luxury resort and private club design experience, Lisa Torbett, ASID, and Dee Simmons, ASID, help homeowners choose furnishings with classic lines, patterns, and colors that simultaneously emulate the resident's personality and goals and the home's architecture. Whatever the final style, Lisa and Dee use their enthusiasm to create a timeless, elegant look.

Above: The bedroom was large enough to accommodate two queen beds, so we added the freeform iron frames for the twin girls' room and repeated the use of iron in the drapery rod. Along with the thin, clean lines of the ironwork, raspberry and coral tones—and the absence of a bed skirt—generate a contemporary, feminine quality without being overwhelming.

Facing Page: Strong color and rich fabrics define the entire vacation home, especially in the grand entertaining space. Paired with the heavy beams, dark stain, and stone floors, every color seems to pop, like the bright tones in the artwork above the bar. Numerous fabric and upholstery patterns play off of each other, lending interest and intrigue through their base hues and a few surprising elements.
Photographs by Howard Lee Puckett

Above: A diagonal layout to the contemporary living area—in the limestone and Spanish tile floor and the placement of the sofa—forges a dramatic statement. The minimal, neutral tones allow the homeowner's fabulous art collection to be the focus. An antique Oushak rug in front of the fireplace and a wool rug under the sofa designate two conversation areas.
Photograph by Howard Lee Puckett

Right: We added a gathered skirt to soften the hard surface of the stone countertop in the quaint but sophisticated powder room. A cream faux-finished wall, silver leaf-edged mirror, and glowing iron sconces are details that complete the soft feel.
Photograph by Luke Hock, 3181 Photography

Facing Page Top: To embrace both a clean ambience and the homeowner's red 1950s-era barstools, we created contrasting colors and tones with minimal accessories. The round mirrors were sourced from water wheels at an old water mill called the Fitz Foundry.
Photograph by Luke Hock, 3181 Photography

Facing Page Bottom: Architectural details—like shaped soffits or archways—help define open-concept spaces and also act as design elements that lessen the need for other accessories and furnishings. If the space lacks strong architectural detail, we often use large sculptures, columns, or screens to act as art on the wall or to give depth to a room.
Photographs by Luke Hock, 3181 Photography

Liza Bryan Interiors

A designer is more than just someone who has good taste; a sense of scale, an understanding of color, and a passion for beautiful things are vital qualities also. Most important, though, is the attribute of being a good editor with the ability to wade through a host of items or ideas and find appropriate ways to use what's important or aesthetically pleasing. For nearly 30 years, Liza Bryan has been embodying these characteristics, gently guiding homeowners through the design process. Probing lifestyle conversations, detailed drawings, and a color and fabric selection process ultimately impart a room or home that respects and showcases the homeowner's interests and collections.

Above Left & Facing Page: Although the style was in complete contrast to most of my designs, I welcomed the challenge to cater to the homeowner's desire for a minimally furnished, modern look in the Peter Block-designed space. A soft palette of cool colors combines with a few surprise hues to offer the perfect backdrop for an art collection. The Vaughan crystal chandelier and ceiling covered in silver tea paper add drama to the dining area; simple elegance in the living room pairs nicely with the impressive coffered ceilings and mahogany windows.

Above Right: In a redesign of an existing home, I focused on updating the colors and organizing the personal furnishings. The impact of a collection is so much greater than a few lovely pieces scattered throughout a home. I freshened the palette to include grey, silver, and blue tones and brought order to the space.
Photographs by Emily Followill

Above & Right: Many times a homeowner has exquisite pieces, but they are placed next to elements that don't mesh well or are just overshadowed by too many furnishings. I edited and rearranged the room to showcase the formal items, including displaying a collection of antique plates around the gilt mirror. The hallway features family heirlooms and invites people into the home. The entire residence is comfortable and classic but not pretentious.
Photographs by Emily Followill

Facing Page: If a homeowner is passionate about a furnishing or artwork, it's my pleasure and honor as a designer to incorporate that item into the room. In the case of a screen, the item can easily be used as an architectural element in the room and wonderfully establishes balance in a large space.
Top photograph by Emily Followill
Bottom photograph by John Umberger

Marjorie Johnston & Co.

For Marjorie Johnston and Wendy Barze, the mother-daughter duo of Marjorie Johnston & Co., the unique style of each project is driven by the combination of their design aesthetic in concert with the homeowner's personal style. By learning about the day-to-day life of the homeowner, discovering individual perceptions of luxury, and finding the items that evoke a gasp of excitement, Marjorie and Wendy take full advantage of their generational differences yet similar design philosophies, collaborating to incorporate interiors that ultimately speak of one thing: the homeowner.

Above: The perfect combination of detail and composition creates memorable interiors. From a custom bolster pillow in linen and cut velvet that completes a guest bedroom to an unexpected arrangement of an antique portrait crowned by an architectural fragment on a foyer console, we strive to incorporate both elegance and whimsy into our interiors.
Left photograph by Miller Mobley
Right photograph by Jean Allsop

Facing Page: Expansive living spaces allow the option to create a room within a room. We used an intimate seating area at the end of a large living room to establish that essence. Vintage club chairs have been reupholstered in plush mohair and are paired with high style lamps, favorite books, and collectibles.
Photograph by Emily Followill

Above & Right: The contrast of contemporary art—a series of studies for a large painting hung together to make a statement—juxtaposed with the commanding portrait illustrate the effect of mixing modern and traditional elements to add interest. We chose the pillows to provide color, pattern, and comfort to the settee. Though the room is clean and crisp, it is also inviting to all who enter. In the foyer, a round painted table anchors the long space; lavender planted in an antique terracotta urn adds a bit of the outdoors, and antique plates for collecting mail and keys provide the practical and the pretty.
Photographs by Jean Allsop

Facing Page Top: Showcasing a collection of items together gives them more weight than if they were spread throughout a home. A collection doesn't have to be a compilation of similar items as long as a common denominator exists, such as color.
Photograph by Emily Followill

Facing Page Bottom: Details like lush fabric or a combination of old and new accessories can bring life to an otherwise ordinary space.
Left photograph by Miller Mobley
Right photograph by Jean Allsop

McLaurin Interiors

In a room, every item should be essential. Begin with and be inspired by things you love. Then, each element should serve a purpose—for color, balance, harmony, or function. This ideal, according to Maria McLaurin Nutt of McLaurin Interiors, leads to spaces that are soothing to the eye as well as to the spirit. Maria combines these meaningful elements with her naturally graceful style to create designs that respectfully mix the old with the new for a warm, inviting ambience.

Above & Facing Page: I tend to organize a room into vignettes to keep it interesting and exciting. In a breakfast room that boasts a 17-foot-high cathedral ceiling and is adjacent to an expansive kitchen, the design needed to have a strong anchor and good balance. A 9- by 12-foot rug establishes a central area, while the fluid lines and graceful curves of the walnut pedestal table reflect the lines of the kitchen island. A second vignette by the entrance from the living room showcases an antique ibis console, which dates back to the American Arts-and-Crafts era. The silk drapery panels soften the architectural lines of the walls and help create a cozy third area with wing chairs.
Photographs by Lauren Rubinstein

Above & Right: Recognizing the beauty of the gardens viewed from the room's windows—which overlook white dogwoods and viburnum—I immediately felt the need for a crisp, clean shade of white for the walls and ceilings of the young lady's space. Soft aquas and creams contrast with youthful yellows to make the room come to life. I mixed old and new not only with the furniture but also with accessories, from the vintage lamps and antique-inspired matelasse coverlet to contemporary lacquered art and a Corbin Bronze sculpture.
Photographs by Chris Little

Facing Page: Flanked by French doors on one side and a walk-through to the contemporary kitchen on the other, the breakfast room required a modern, graphic edge. Beginning with the Lorraine Christie painting, which was the inspiration for the color and ambience of the space, I then selected graceful, high-backed chairs and covered them in a silk-linen blend fabric to surround the pristine acrylic-based table. A hand-forged iron console in silver leaf complements the space. A balance of graphic lines and soft curves with contrasting textures and colors express a sense of serene harmony.
Photograph by Lauren Rubinstein

Monday's House of Design

A home should be celebrated for its central function within family life. The best avenue to achieve this honor is through comprehensive design, which integrates every component of the home and every request of the homeowner. Lynn Monday takes this idea and then transforms spaces with rich details, balance, color, and texture, while simultaneously accounting for the function of the room. Her designs are at once luxurious and inviting.

Above & Facing Page: An urban home called for refined glamour, elegance, and comfort, which was inspired by the silk Osborne & Little window treatments. The fabric's black, champagne, and taupe tones extend throughout the living area; a pop of pink and a leopard print bring electric details into the space. The leather sofa and chenille lounge chair add textural interest. Antique pieces, like the chest and cabinet, are grounded by a few contemporary accents of art and accessories.
Photographs by Chris Little Photography

"The secret to creating a beautiful room is to make it elegant, inviting, functional, and comfortable." *Lynn Monday*

Above: A designer is not only helpful in completely renovating a room, but can also take existing furnishings and revolutionize a space. In the library, the homeowner already had purchased most of the elements. I moved the furniture around to create visual interest. The refined linen window treatments add height and softness to the wood walls, and the custom pillows add texture and shape to the sofa.

Facing Page: The wife's original concept for the kitchen involved a white tone-on-tone ambience, but our collaboration with Design Galleria led us to a mix of hues and surfaces. Stainless steel appliances as well as stainless steel drawer fronts add a modern edge to the formal Carrara marble countertops. The husband loved the hint of purple in the countertop, so we added custom chairs with a Cowtan & Tout Montego fabric in lilas on the front, light stone-colored linen on the back, and silver nailhead trim.
Photographs by Chris Little Photography

Nancy Price Interior Design

Contrasting elements are essential to a room's design, yet they require an acute appreciation for the individual characteristics as well as the connection among them. Nancy Price learned how to aptly weave a study in contrast into a space from her architectural background, a personal passion for art, and more than 20 years in the industry. Through a layering process, the firm of Nancy Price Interior Design transfers the vision and lifestyle of each homeowner into thoughtful, alluring vignettes. Whether a sleek, modern home in Malibu or a traditional French residence in the South, every project expresses appropriate scale, function, and beauty.

Above & Facing Page: Deep in the heart of the Mississippi Delta, the home's open floorplan is perfect for entertaining. I was inspired by the sheer scale of the antique French gilt mirror procured on a buying trip and knew it would be perfect for the dining room. The mirror perfectly complements and reflects the room's other design elements, including the consoles made of old French balustrades, the beautiful polished dining table, and the large French chandelier. The exterior back porch was repurposed into an interior loggia where I combined old and new for a sophisticated atmosphere. The contrast between the plaster walls with beautiful antique doors installed as art and the clean lines of the custom chairs is striking. A pair of captivating lanterns produces gorgeous damask-like shadows on the ceiling at night.
Photographs by James Patterson Photography

Above & Facing Page Bottom: The pool and poolhouse are an extension of the home, and I felt it was important to bring the same aesthetic over using materials that are conducive to indoor-outdoor living. The concrete sofa with concrete bolsters offers a logical, functional design element that balances the structure of the poolhouse. Inside, limestone tile flooring and durable fabrics delineate elegance with functionality. The intricacy of the 18th-century shell fragment mirror enhances the modern dining environment. Sheer draperies and backless custom benches allow a comfortable, original atmosphere.

Facing Page Top: The main salon is gently embraced by wooden columns with a beautiful patina that provide contrast to the more formal settee. Soft blue tones from the dining room were continued through upholstery on the settee and in the aged Oushak rug for a cohesive look. To give life to a console the clients loved, we repurposed it into an elegant coffee table.
Photographs by James Patterson Photography

"A marriage of opposites—modern elements with antique pieces—highlights both their individuality and compatibility." *Nancy Price*

Richard Tubb Interiors

It's not at all unusual for a group of ladies to wander into Richard Tubb Interiors and say with a smile that they've simply come to enjoy the ambience. Because people always keep things longer than they intend to, designers Richard Tubb, Sean Beam, and David Walker like to create rooms that can easily be redressed on a whim. To accomplish this goal, they tend to specify major features as solids and use minor elements to introduce a bit of pattern or color. While they definitely like to stylistically mix things up, they are always mindful to design timelessly and be good stewards of homeowners' funds, whether outfitting a modest family home or an elaborate vacation property.

Above: Like a timeworn strand of pearls, the most elegant rooms often possess a rich array of creams and whites. Designed for a family of four, the elegant living room isn't treated as a museum; it's enjoyed daily, as family members read, lounge, and visit with one another. The owners acquired the pair of contemporary paintings several years before we designed their home but never displayed the artwork, so they were delighted that we made the paintings figure so prominently. Design isn't about seeing how many new things you can acquire, it's about using great pieces in unexpected ways.

Facing Page: Furnishings, fabrics, and accents are simply the tools we use to create a sense of place. The daybed niche establishes a relaxing tone at the entrance to the master suite, so whether the owners spend time in the space or just enjoy the visual as they pass by, it serves a beautiful purpose. Design by Richard Tubb.
Photographs by Mitchell Sargent

Above: Whenever possible and appropriate, we like to specify the creations of Southern artists and craftsmen, whose unique pieces and meaningful stories lend homes a sense of romance and intrigue. Something as simple as a side table with interesting lines really helps to keep your eye flowing throughout the space, eager to discover other special touches.
Photograph by Mitchell Sargent

Facing Page: When we're designing various rooms in a home, they read as variations on a theme for a smooth flow with eye-catching focal points throughout. The living room of a home in Birmingham was incredibly long and a bit awkward so rather than forcing the whole room together, we visually divided it into two seating areas and united it with a wonderfully textural sisal rug. Because the owners had quite a few incredible antiques and works of art, we kept the colors soft and soothing. In the bedroom, a thick shag carpet anchors the space, and yards and yards of a lightly patterned stripe frame the windows and the luxurious bed. From afar, the fabrics read as solids but up close, they have beautiful patterns that feel very boutique and special. Design by Sean Beam and David Walker.
Photographs by Sylvia Martin

"Possessing simplicity and ease, a home should be the calm center of a family's universe." *Richard Tubb*

Robert Brown Interior Design

Robert Brown's first love—fashion—is instantly evident in the smart, refined interior designs for which he's so well known. With experience of more than two decades in the fashion industry, Robert can't help but be drawn to exquisite fabrics with unrivaled details and to magnificent color, which he says truly sets the mood. Now more than a decade into capturing the essence of homeowners in their spaces, Robert's spaces embrace a mix of styles—traditional with contemporary, a modern painting over a fabulous French commode—to enhance the residents' lifestyle.

Above: A beautiful, serene shade of blue subtly washes the background of a gallery's transition space to encourage visitors to relax and enjoy the art. In the furnishings, I mimicked a few subtle Greek details from the photos to deftly influence a classic feel among the modern atmosphere.

Facing Page: Traditional and up-to-date aren't exclusive concepts in interior design; both ideas can be expressed. In a living room, I infused a very modern painting into the time-honored ambience of antique furnishings and formal finishes. The neutral palette enables the painting to become a wonderful juxtaposition to the French chairs and the new limestone fireplace, also reminiscent of a soft, French style.
Photographs by Chris Little Photography

Above: An eclectic art collection can speak for itself when surrounded by a neutral color palette. Variety within the textures—a velvet sofa, wool rug, and the chair's herringbone pattern—connects the furnishings, and a macabre vibe and similar hues lend a commonality to the art.

Facing Page Top: In the living room of a Tuscan home in Atlanta, furniture placement was key to ensure the correct balance and scale were achieved in relation to the 22-foot ceilings and nearly eight-foot-tall fireplace. I created three seating areas, unified with a large sisal rug and a tone-on-tone color scheme. The traditional but clean ambience was executed with a mix of antique and contemporary accessories, minimal in number.

Facing Page Bottom: Surrounded by a pale platinum wall and champagne upholstery, the living area establishes a thoughtful ambience, offering accessories and furnishings from a variety of historical periods. I repeated an ebony hue around the room to continually keep the eye landing on something new.
Photographs by Chris Little Photography

"Design is a construction process, layering element upon element as we go." *Robert Brown*

C. Weaks Interiors

Carole Weaks is innately drawn to the combination of antique furniture and contemporary art. It works well in every setting and creates a timeless aesthetic that people of all stylistic bents can appreciate. Carole values antiques for their classic lines, craftsmanship, history, and one-of-a-kind essence. She's passionate about contemporary artwork—not the "shock value" pieces commonly associated with the genre, but rather the thoughtfully made pieces—because of the emotional responses they elicit. When introducing people to contemporary art and accompanying them on shopping excursions, her requirements are simple: The piece must bring them joy and speak to them on a personal level. Even the most avid traditionalists find themselves pleasantly surprised by the juxtaposition of old and new.

Above & Facing Page: Who would have thought that two antique mirrors could act as architectural elements? Flanking the fireplace, the mirrors look like they were meant for the space, adding wonderful depth and interest. Reflected in the mirrors, antique tables—one gilded wood, the other hand-forged iron—hold beautiful sculptures that are punctuated by boldly colored contemporary paintings. I chose the racetrack-shaped table for its easy edges and surrounded it with chairs upholstered in Nancy Corzine fabrics. The silk draperies and authentic Oushak rug are elegant yet neutral backdrops to the art and furnishings. The variety of elements and styles is really quite striking, and it proves that if you're true to your taste in every design selection you make, somehow all of the elements will work together.
Photographs by Emily Followill

Carolyn Hultman Interior Design

Envisioning the finished room before the project has begun is the surest way to avoid mistakes and guarantee the end result is a thoughtful, functional ambience that illustrates the homeowner's lifestyle. For Carolyn Hultman, this concept is second nature. As soon as she enters a room, she immediately devises multiple ways to redesign the space. Of course, her ideas are adjusted as necessary throughout the design process, but often her initial vision is the perfect culmination of the residents' personalities, the room's purpose, and a relaxing yet classic style that will endure for years to come.

Above: The 19th-century home retains much of its original architecture and sophistication, including wonderful mouldings and stunning chandeliers. I used a mix of antiques and contemporary pieces to blend the family's appreciation for history and a modern lifestyle. A painted glass tabletop and antique chairs with metal handles offer a lovely office space next to an oversized window with direct access to the patio. In the living room, the original chandelier was the starting point for the color palette; an antique console table and early 20th-century carved wooden candelabra are juxtaposed with the sisal carpet.

Facing Page: I embraced neutral tones throughout the home to lend a calming ambience and provide a subtle backdrop for the homeowner's fabulous art collection. The original mahogany newel posts and railings establish an impressive entry that is continued with tortoise shells used as art and a variety of materials—metal stools and lamp, leather cushions, pottery, a sturdy rug, and a tortoise-shell parsons table.
Photographs by Deborah Whitlaw Llewellyn

Evon Kirkland Interiors

Balance. Serenity. Function. Clean. An Evon Kirkland interior will not shock—it will soothe the soul and make you want to linger, to find comfort in that place called home. A design by Evon Kirkland McAngus begins with a neutral background. Clean, atmospheric palettes allow her to use color as an accessory and to immediately set a tone that embraces balance and beauty.

Above & Facing Page: The classic home is only minutes from downtown, but its location on a quiet cul-de-sac makes the city fade into the distance. If the kitchen is the heart, the areas adjoining this home's kitchen are its soul. Graciously proportioned, the breakfast room opens on to a handsome loggia—a favorite place to relax with family and friends. The husband is an outdoorsman, so I represented his love of the South Carolina Low Country in the breakfast table base, which is crafted of a cypress tree trunk. Her career in fashion shows up in the delightful dressmaker detailing of the upholstered, button-back chairs. Framed large-scale botanicals by a local artist, juxtaposed with a pair of modern cowhide ottomans, add to the whimsical integrity of the space. Comfortable and inviting, the room is the perfect escape.
Photographs by Rick Smoak

Knotting Hill Interiors

Kimberly Grigg has an innate creative energy that was seen first when she was just six years old as she hired neighborhood boys to paint her bedroom walls. Ever since, she has found great pleasure in designing and creating appropriate rooms, first with her event design firm that created beautiful spaces for special occasions and now through Knotting Hill Interiors. Whatever the locale—waterfront, mountain, or metropolitan—or the design style—traditional, modern, or an eclectic mix—Kimberly insists on comfortable interiors, and believes that those spaces can, and should, be aesthetically pleasing. Most importantly, she is known for generating a plethora of exceptional ideas.

Above: Through a two-year renovation, I was both the designer and general contractor, creating a finely accessorized home with lush textiles and copious layers. Instead of paneling, it seemed a great idea to use handsome masculine toile on the walls to lend an air of quiet sophistication next to exquisite drapery. Plaques and pictures hang from the bookcase and add a sense of surprise. In the master suite, where a blue ceiling evokes a French atrium-like feel, a bed commissioned from Italy is topped with luxurious layers.

Facing Page: A French trumeau mirror layered on top of another mirror sets the tone for the fine living room. The roundabout settee was originally used as extra seating for a party, but it suited the room perfectly so I kept it in the space. The entire room has pattern upon pattern and texture upon texture; even the neutral wall color is overlaid with a hand-stenciled damask pattern.
Photographs by Carl Kerridge Photography

Lisa Torbett Interiors, page 228

Judy Bentley Interior Views, page 224

Mary-Bryan Peyer Designs, page 210

Todd Richesin Interiors, page 256

Ginger Brewton Interiors

To prevent a space from feeling stale, Ginger Brewton invokes an eclectic mix of antique and modern pieces. Whether she recovers an antique chair with a contemporary fabric or installs funky wallpaper in a room with traditional furnishings, Ginger believes balancing the aesthetic feel in a room achieves a soothing, elegant effect. This style of design requires a keen eye to ensure everything coordinates correctly—something at which Ginger certainly excels. Whether she's working on a relaxed coastal home or a modern loft in the city, Ginger's inspiration is derived from the homeowner, her numerous years in the design industry, and nearly everything around her.

Above & Facing Page: Rearing six children necessitates a sense of calm and order in the design. Because of the home's proximity to the water, my goal was to bring the outside ambience in. The homeowners loved my selection of the aqua grasscloth wallpaper for the master bedroom. Layering the window treatments—with a sheer fabric underneath a patterned, blackout-lined fabric in the master bedroom and a light-filtering shade with sheer drapery in the living area—establishes an airy, simple atmosphere.
Photographs by Bill Bennett, Workhorse Images

Above & Facing Page Bottom Right: In the girls' bedroom and bath, I wanted to impart a sense of youth and playfulness, but still maintain the calming atmosphere evident in the rest of the home. Neutral tones on the walls, drapery, and furnishings set the serene ambience, while the pink hues exclaim a feminine lightheartedness. Curtains around each bunk bed allow each young lady her own privacy. The bathroom came together perfectly with the homeowner's settee, which features hot pink buttons. I coordinated the accent tile with the settee's green tone.

Facing Page Top: The kitchen and dining area form a functional, pleasing space that can withstand constant use. I found a dining table with a zinc surface, which will increase in character over time. The chair fabric features the tan hue from the living room and gives off a soft essence next to the linen sheers. Just as durable as granite, the crushed-shell countertop is light in color and helps bring the outside in.

Facing Page Bottom Left: In the boy's bathroom, where the window wasn't functional because of the faucet's placement, I hung a useful but decorative mirror from an antique doorknob to better utilize the space and add a touch of whimsy.

Photographs by Bill Bennett, Workhorse Images

Top Left: Neighboring the family's large plantation house, the homeowners wanted to build a structure reminiscent of a large screened porch where everyone could hang out. They wanted everything to blend in with the surroundings, to feel as if you were outside yet protected from the elements. The architect's result is a stunning open-air space that features copper window screens in place of glass panes. Although the space is covered from direct sun and rain, I still had to keep in mind the moisture in the air when selecting furnishings. Teak furniture and water-resistant fabric, along w th mostly neutral tones, ensure the furniture's longevity.

Middle & Bottom Left: In keeping with the natural essence of the space, the bar's counter was crafted from a tree that had been removed from the property. The homeowners also interjected a personal touch in the bathroom, where oyster shells that they had collected were infused into the sink basin. Many of the light fixtures, courtesy of the architect, appear as if they are floating; they gently sway in the breeze.

Facing Page: Since the family frequently entertains, durability is of the utmost importance; no one wants to worry about harming the furnishings. The solution was found in an enduring stained-concrete dining table and sturdy metal chairs.
Photographs by Wendy Cooper

Mary-Bryan Peyer Designs

Without order, a home can't provide the restful sanctuary that it should. To achieve the harmonious ambience, Mary-Bryan Peyer and her diversely talented team embrace the well-known saying, "A place for everything and everything in its place." Whether implementing a room-by-room redesign or starting from scratch at the blueprint stage, Mary-Bryan expresses her penchant for a clean look by blending classic Southern style with contemporary flair. A focus on the homeowner's lifestyle—needs, wants, and functionality—versus a trend or specific style, leads to more satisfying, timeless designs.

Above: We created a light, airy feeling to direct the focus toward the unequaled vistas of the California-style home overlooking a spectacular marsh and gorgeous live oak trees. The family room, dining area, and kitchen—all leading out to the pool—reflect a slightly casual feeling through lively fabric with a few bold colors. The vaulted ceiling and its natural-tone beams add interest without weight. For continuity, the antique silver steel finish on the dining area's light fixture complements the working brackets on the trusses.

Facing Page: In the sitting room just inside the front entry, we subtly embraced an indoor-outdoor connection to draw the eye into the home. A jute rug, raffia-like fabric on the ottoman, bamboo floor lamps, a rusted iron side table with concrete top, and muted hues take their cues from natural elements. The window sheers are luxurious without hindering the light or views.
Photographs by Ben Galland, H20 Creative Group

Above & Right: The empty nesters' incredible collection of Native American artifacts was the inspiration for their lakeside retreat. Blended with the Mediterranean architecture of the home, the art expresses immense history and injects great texture and color. To emphasize the beautiful ceiling, we used warm wood pieces in the formal living room and dining room—an antique desk as a sofa table and a rich dining table with antique chairs.

Facing Page Top & Bottom Left: In the seaside home's formal living space, we wanted to maximize seating and provide two focal points: one on the fireplace and one toward the adjacent dining room. The homeowner's plethora of beautiful antiques provided a perfect jumping-off point for the space; we highlighted her majolica plate collection in two bookshelves—incorporating a shell design in the top—and carried the colors throughout the room. A soft, subtle chartreuse linen herringbone pattern combines well with the fun, traditional print on the club chairs and the French bergère.

Facing Page Bottom Right: We enclosed the porch to create a casual, airy sunroom to comfortably enjoy the beautiful pool and marshland views. The homeowner's stunning green armoire confirmed the color palette and nicely coordinates with the nearby living room. Cypress walls are slightly whitewashed for a calming aesthetic; the cedar-planked ceiling is painted a tone similar to the sofa's muted blue color.
Photographs by Ben Galland, H20 Creative Group

Above & Right: Working with the homeowners—who requested a blue and white space—and the architect, we agreed that the bustling family needed a child-friendly space that was still sophisticated. The master bedroom became a serene, quiet escape with soft prints in a comfortable seating area, a soothing wool rug, mirrored bedside tables for a bit of glamour, and double window treatments for style and functionality. In the front stair hall, a blue and white dhurrie rug boasts an ethnic pattern and contrasts nicely with the custom bamboo table base and the traditional Chinese jug jar.

Facing Page: To frame the living and dining areas, we used a mixture of natural and hand-painted and -sanded pecky cypress and smooth cypress for the exposed woodwork. We played with the home's seaside location by adding a tabby wall—a traditional construction of crushed shells, cement, and sand—around the fireplace. White linen slipcovers, graphic print down pillows, and an Asian weaver's table used as a durable coffee table impart a comfortable atmosphere. The pine dining table, which easily seats 10, and the French antique chandelier above are the perfect pair of simplicity and elegance.
Photographs by Ben Galland, H2O Creative Group

Carolyn Hultman Interior Design

It's wise to invest in one classic black dress instead of four trendy ones. Relating fashion to her longtime love, Carolyn Hultman applies this same concept to the design of a home. By choosing timeless, progressive style over fads that come and go, a home can be relevant for numerous generations, providing a relaxing, comfortable space. The bones of a well-planned house or the lines of a quality piece of furniture are some of the elements Carolyn likes to start with, first by appreciating the original design and then reinvigorating the environment with a fresh take on the traditional.

Above: A Shingle-style home called for a touch of that same rustic elegance on the inside. The dining room features a sleek copper bartop, a glass table, and clean lines in the persimmon leather barstools next to an exposed brick archway and sliding barn doors. I illustrated the homeowner's personality and preferences through the earth palette of green, brown, and persimmon tones, which originated from a dish the homeowner purchased in Italy.

Facing Page: The architectural elements in the living room are simply amazing, so I highlighted them through a variety of finishes: one washed upper wall, one painted upper wall, rustic shutters, dark beams, exposed brick, supple leather, and a sisal carpet. A few contemporary finishes—nailhead trim on the chairs, glass and metal coffee table, rectangular lampshades—inject an updated feel to the space.
Photographs by Deborah Whitlaw Llewellyn

Above Left & Bottom Left: Botanical prints and embroidered leaf detail on the drapery in both the architecturally savvy master bedroom and the bright, feminine office space bring the outside in.

Above Right: Not solely functional, the master bathroom exudes a thoughtful ambience with striking details. I love how the soaking tub fits perfectly in the niche and is accented by a lively metallic tile border. The detail in the custom cabinets adds elegance, while the simple glazed finish subtly speaks to the home's rustic nature.

Facing Page Top: Just off the dining room, the screened-in dining porch overlooks a lap pool, the river, and the marsh beyond. Perennial outdoor fabrics in similar tones to those inside maintain a smooth flow from indoors to out.

Facing Page Bottom: While still tying the design to the rest of the home through the rustic beams, I animated the media room with a fun chartreuse and orange print on the linen drapery and accent pillow. A cork ceiling, chartreuse glass lamps, and a sturdy wood and metal coffee table make the most of the design.
Photographs by Deborah Whitlaw Llewellyn

Evon Kirkland Interiors

The homeowners that Evon Kirkland McAngus partners with are a loyal lot; many have been with her for over a decade. They appreciate her attention to detail, the time she spends listening to their wants and needs, and her concern that each home reflect their lifestyle. The end result is a space that feels like a sanctuary, a sigh of relief at the end of a busy day.

Above & Facing Page: A spectacular lakefront residence presented the opportunity to work with the homeowners throughout the process from groundbreaking to moving day. With such a location, the goal was to create a dynamic home that took full advantage of its special point on the water. The graceful curve of the staircase opens to a living area that offers unobstructed views of the lake beyond. I suggested a subdued color scheme with the result being a tone of quiet and tranquility. The seating is functional, a twist on the classics, and takes no attention away from the drama of the water. The dining room features a table from Councill and Henredon dining chairs that have been covered in a Sunbrella fabric. Suddenly, a cream-colored fabric dining chair doesn't seem like such a folly.
Photographs by Rick Smoak

Above & Left: In the family room, I deepened the neutral colors a few shades to create a warmer, enveloping space. A wooden tray ceiling adds another layer of depth and comfort. Closed doors along one wall open to reveal everything the homeowners might want in entertainment. On the opposite side of the entry, the home office features custom iron doors, trimmed in a rich mahogany that is echoed in the room's paneled ceiling.

Facing Page: On the upper level, the rooms' designs took their cue from the structurally required beams. With a bit of an Old English feel to them, the home theater and game room offer alternative entertaining opportunities for the couple's teenage daughters. But the wall of windows reminds that the lake is waiting just outside.
Photographs by Rick Smoak

"Timeless, sophisticated choices for major furnishings help create a space that the homeowner will appreciate and fall in love with." *Evon Kirkland McAngus*

Judy Bentley Interior Views

Inspiration doesn't necessarily have to come from an observed physical object or even an item in the present. For Judy Bentley, owner of Interior Views, inspiration is a blend of the homeowner's style and personality mixed with her own experience and knowledge. Through her understanding of fabrics, rugs, furniture, and color, as well as her ability to visualize the space and punctuate the details, Judy's inspiration is transformed into designs that lean toward the traditional but include a little pizzazz to reflect an inviting, timeless essence.

Above: Naturally, homes overlooking the water call for a more relaxed feel than those in the city. In a waterfront condominium on Hilton Head Island, I embraced the surroundings by establishing a masculine yacht-like feel in the office area with prints of boats, palm tree fabric on the comfortable chairs, and lanterns that I turned into electric lamps. Antique scotch barrels reflect the husband's affinity for the drink.

Facing Page: The guest room in the condo was inspired by the wicker furniture and by my intense fondness for blue and white. As soon as I saw the fabric, I knew it was the perfect choice and would succinctly punctuate the space along with the purchased shell collection.
Photographs by Erica George Dines

Above & Right: Inspiration sprung from the homeowner's childhood in Panama where a British West Indies vibe was rampant in the designs. I generated that same feel in the master bedroom through the dark wood, window shutters, and a four-poster bed, but kept the lightness with neutral surfaces. The guest bedroom features a few pieces of pottery from a Virginia artisan, an antique drop-leaf table, and antique palm prints.

Facing Page: The main living area of the Hilton Head condo continues the relaxed feel through warm colors and lots of seating to accommodate guests. I covered the main pieces of furniture in chocolate brown and cream ticking and accented with red tones. The large dining table is handsomely accented by the simple lines of the chandelier, which offers a nice scale but doesn't take away from the view. The French doors lead out to an ample covered terrace where guests can relax on the palm tree-inspired wicker furniture and enjoy the gorgeous water views while remaining protected from the elements.
Photographs by Erica George Dines

Lisa Torbett Interiors

The entire essence of a room should make a pleasant impression as soon as someone enters the space, without the feeling that one element is dominating the room. To achieve this, Lisa Torbett, ASID, and Dee Simmons, ASID, co-owners of Lisa Torbett Interiors, embrace a clean, transitional aesthetic where the furnishings and accessories coexist nicely yet still embody a remarkable quality. Through the perfect blend of comfort, sophistication, and timelessness, their inspiring rooms appropriately reflect the lovely views outside.

Above: To visually distinguish between the open-concept spaces of the kitchen and living-dining area, an archway with antique light fixtures highlights the island and an accent tile motif draws the eye into the room. The light tones of the cabinets and countertops allow the cypress island and oak floors to really stand out. We utilized textured wall surfaces to illustrate the Mediterranean architecture of the upscale, coastal townhome.

Facing Page: The sitting room and breakfast nook overlooking the water exude an airy, coastal feel that is fun and inviting. While traditional elements are interspersed amidst the clean lines of the sofa and fairly neutral tones, the pizzazz is found in the 1940s Segal tapestry on the wall, the unique candle chandelier, and the one-of-a-kind footstool.
Photographs by Luke Hock, 3181 Photography

Above: A slight Bohemian theme gradually took place in the screened porch as plaster walls, a raised hearth, and limestone floors gave way to antique iron wall sconces, relaxed seating, and a round woven coffee table. The homeowner—who is also a builder—continued the Gothic arch from the screened openings into the fireplace.
Photograph by John Umberger

Facing Page: Painting ceiling timbers white is a pragmatic yet refined way of bringing the relaxed beach ambience inside; creating a tone-on-tone space allows for the dramatic views to take the spotlight. We then added in other elements, like a 10-foot solid teak dining table paired with a colorful banquette or a combination of numerous geometric patterns, for a subtly piquant aesthetic.
Photographs by Luke Hock, 3181 Photography

"An overall design or a specific accessory isn't something you should be talked into. You should fall in love as soon as you see it."
Dee Simmons

Liza Bryan Interiors

The color palette in a room should welcome people into the space, gently guiding them in to enjoy the ambience. For Liza Bryan Interiors, this idea translates into a beautifully designed room that avoids any single element that might jump out to disrupt the flow. The welcoming, smooth design can be achieved through soft, neutral tones that are easy to live with and provide a wonderful backdrop for more vibrant accessories that are effortlessly changed to reflect current tastes or styles. Through unrivaled thoughtfulness and a thorough approach, Liza lends her impeccable knowledge and sense of style for a handsome, refined effect.

Above: A house on Lake Burton was designed by Keith Summerour as an authentic Adirondack home. The portiere curtains around the arched opening in the entrance hall suggest a surprise waiting in the next room. The river-recovered cypress walls in the lodge room beyond exude warmth and comfort, creating the perfect background for items that mirror the past but are usable for today, such as the replica hooked rug.
Photographs by Mali Azima

Facing Page: The kitchen in a St. Simons Island residence epitomizes the feeling of the entire home: modern amenities hidden in matured materials generate great texture—including a variety of aged finishes, from a pecky cypress ceiling and a zinc island countertop to quartersawn vintage flooring and hand-hewn reclaimed beams.
Photograph by Luke Hock

Above: A huge outdoor space appears warm and friendly with its old brick floor, twig furniture, and a different tartan throw on the back of each chair for guests to stay cozy.
Photograph by Luke Hock

Facing Page Left: In the St. Simons home, each bedroom has its own personality and appears as if it jumped out from the past. In one room, board and batten and lovely wallpaper are joined to the painted ship-lap board ceiling with grosgrain ribbon. Window cornices are fashioned from twigs and allow the curtains to be drawn. The homeowner loved the pumpkin color, so I used the hue in another bedroom with charcoal and cream accents for a neutral base. The custom heart pine four-poster beds create individual sleeping areas.
Photographs by Luke Hock

Facing Page Top Right: In an Adirondack lakehouse guest room, a Martha Washington reproduction chair is dressed down with cotton ticking upholstery.
Photograph by Mali Azima

Facing Page Bottom Right: Designed so the homeowner could relax in her claw foot tub and gaze out over the lake, the bathroom features river-recovered cypress walls and a heart pine floor. The Oriental rug adds the finishing touch to the space.
Photograph by Luke Hock

"A casual look comes from paying attention to the details." *Liza Bryan*

Marjorie Johnston & Co.

Marjorie Johnston and Wendy Barze of Marjorie Johnston & Co. have been taught by experience that the home is defined by who lives there. No matter the scope of the project, the challenge in designing is to interpret and fulfill the homeowner's vision through the choices of fabrics, furnishings, and accessories. A sense of place is always a consideration when designing in specific locales, like the beach or the mountains. Rooms should be suitable and comfortable, while simultaneously exhibiting a classic, fresh design with unexpected twists. At the core of every project, a subtle Southern aesthetic prevails, living casually with fine things.

Above: The homeowner has an incredible collection of marvelous turquoise china. Instead of hiding it away in a cupboard, we allowed it to be both useful and aesthetically pleasing through its display in nearly every room of the coastal condominium.

Facing Page: The appearance of the homeowner's china continues the rhythm in the large living area. Its fresh, clean look makes the elegant antiques stand out. Original brass hardware on the serpentine chest and the 19th-century French mirror set the stage for the composition of accessories that can be changed and moved to take on a different feel.
Photographs by Miller Mobley

Above & Left: Wonderful curves, soft linen velvet textured fabric, and a few signature pillows on the sofa beg guests to sit down and relax. To add a touch of whimsy to the room, a fun Louis Vuitton footstool was used. Objects on the coffee table play to the locale without being too cliché, and an open shelving system provides a display opportunity while concealing the television.

Facing Page Top & Bottom: We always encourage our homeowners to have fresh, natural elements in every room. In the entrance and dining room, fresh flowers and fruit provide color and scent, making the rooms come alive.

Facing Page Middle: The fabric pattern commands the room and ties in with the home's color palette. Two sunburst mirrors are used as a pair above the bamboo headboards. The boldly colored linen stools at the end of each bed are useful for luggage or as a place to perch.
Photographs by Miller Mobley

Monday's House of Design

As Lynn Monday begins to transform a space into the intriguing look that she and the homeowners desire, the design unfolds in her mind as if she were watching a film. From the opening scene of various elements and ideas, Lynn can envision the room coming to life, telling a story about those who live within its walls. Through engaging her traditionalist style and embracing her creative edge, Lynn takes that vision and establishes well-articulated spaces for the most discriminating homeowners.

Above & Facing Page: My inspiration came from the Caribbean art with its carefree, relaxing ambience that's full of color and life. The sun-kissed feeling of the outdoors and the gorgeous beaches are seen with the white tones, while the ocean is brought in with the hints of turquoise. The hot pink and orange color adds an unexpected jolt that gives life to the space and keeps it fresh. Well-placed accessories give a sophisticated look to seashells and fish-shaped candlesticks, which are personal and meaningful.
Photographs by Chris Little Photography

Above & Facing Page: In the breakfast area where the sun generously pours in during the morning, a sisal rug begins the delicate balance of tone and texture. A sage green hue on the walls doesn't refract light, so the paint can bring a sense of tranquility to the space. White upholstered furniture is appropriately juxtaposed against the aged, green French cane-back chairs. I painted the reproduction side table in a high-gloss white and repurposed it as a tea table. Ferns growing just outside the window are mirrored in the pillows and art.
Photographs by Chris Little Photography

"Every room is like a painting; color, texture, shape, and lighting give life and personality."
Lynn Monday

Nancy Price Interior Design

A home is a sanctuary. A place to relax, to accommodate both the dearest friends and family and the newest acquaintances. A place of peace. For Nancy Price, founder and principal of her eponymous firm, a restful residence is created through visually interesting—and often contrasting—pieces that coexist in just the right balance. She and her team establish neutral "bones" first, then layer in art, textiles, and accessories, many times selected from their global showroom. At the heart of creating a residential haven are the homeowners and their lifestyle; every design choice is based on a personal relationship.

Above: A neutral palette and minimal designs on the walls and floors offer the art and accessories the chance to stand on their own within the Italianate home. In the dining room, a mixture of sleek versus texture, curves versus straight lines, contemporary art versus Renaissance adds intrigue. Brazilian rochester chairs flanking the fireplace expand the room's usefulness into both a dining and sitting area.

Facing Page: Placed between a lovely courtyard and a contemporary kitchen, the casual dining area gently plays with modern and antique pieces. I used the antique element of the Tabernacle table base to allow a fusion of design and formal beauty to be created. The ethereal cobweb-colored sheers complete the room.
Photographs by James Patterson Photography

Above & Left: I treated the kitchen as a living area—a space to be embraced rather than hidden—by selecting an island that resembles an altar table and adding elegant chandeliers and beautiful accessories. A velvet, vintage-style sofa and layered rugs are distinctly set apart with the contemporary Lucite tables. Throughout the home, the neutral background allows the beautiful art and religious reliquaries to speak for themselves.

Facing Page Top: The master bedroom continues the representation of contrasting elements. A spectacular gilded mirror, once part of a formal ballroom in a Buenos Aires mansion, now speaks volumes in relation to the contemporary elements such as the acrylic pedestal, the Italian glass cabinet, and the primitive but elegant cowhide rug. The paneled wood wall opens to reveal a hidden office area.

Facing Page Bottom: A curved wall in the master bathroom creates movement necessary for a fluid, unique design. I displayed personal treasures on the bookcase in a disciplined yet artful composition, while the masculine lines of the Savonarola chair mimic the curved walls.
Photographs by James Patterson Photography

Sarah Jones Interiors

Upon walking into a home designed under the keen eyes of Sarah Nelson, Allied Member ASID—the founder and principal of Sarah Jones Interiors—and her associate, Catherine Graeber, no one would be able to pinpoint who had directed the decorating process. The spaces would exude the personality and charm of the homeowner and would be well-organized and refined, with the design taking advantage of each room's greatest attributes. However, the home's particular style wouldn't necessarily point to Sarah or Catherine. And that is exactly how they prefer to work. They don't want their own expression to be left behind; instead, they want each residence to exquisitely reflect those living within its walls.

Above & Facing Page: A classic home in the country, designed by architect Ken Tate, embraces a Federal vernacular that we continued inside through traditional furnishings and accessories, as well as a symmetrical arrangement. The homeowner's numerous 100-year-old Oriental rugs also dictated the feel of the design on the first floor. Sophisticated, airy fabrics and colors—such as the buttery-yellow tone on the walls—forge a calm ambience to coordinate with the bustling patterns in the rugs and chosen décor. A few splashes of a lovely verdant hue, in addition to the focus on the large windows, maintain the natural atmosphere and bring the outdoors in.
Photographs by Tom Joynt

"Good design begins with the home's location." *Sarah Nelson*

Above: To incorporate a bit of the home's location in a beautiful rural area, we infused a few subtle country chic touches into the classic home. The entryway boasts a sophisticated paisley pattern on the Fortuny material that we selected for the crescent table. Miniature topiaries generate height and give a nod to the grand estates of yesteryear. Another space on the first floor of the home showcases the original brickwork, set off by a traditionally framed piece of art and a cherry console table. An ensconced candle invokes a romantic feel.
Photographs by Tom Joynt

Facing Page: In a bedroom, luxurious linens and well-planned artwork make all the difference in comfort and style. We imparted a layered look in the master bedroom to tone down the formality and increase the warmth. Monogrammed pillows top off the fluffy collection on the bed. A combination of stripes and solids ensures interest, while the small range of colors prevents the bedroom and adjoining sitting area from becoming too busy. The guest bedroom exudes a slightly more refined feel while still welcoming visitors. Appropriately sized end tables and lamps are both functional and aesthetically pleasing.
Top photograph by Tom Joynt
Bottom photograph by Hubert Worley

Southern Studio Interior Design

Every room should evoke a specific emotion or speak to the heart. Whether it's through a calming ambience of muted colors or a striking piece of art that stirs the soul, every element plays a role. For Vicky Serany, founder and principal of Southern Studio Interior Design, of even greater importance than the individual pieces that make up the room are the people who will live in it. A key to the firm's success is the emphasis on careful observation of lifestyle and personality. Once-average rooms are transformed into beautiful spaces that are both functional and comfortable, but most importantly, a home.

Above Left: An active family wanted a casual, comfortable home for a weekend retreat. I created a sophisticated but unpretentious ambience that hinted at a bright, airy lodge. Adjacent the kitchen, the family gathers in the keeping room, which features a table that can be raised for eating or playing games or lowered for use as a coffee table.

Above Right: A generous circular table—featuring a lazy Susan for accessibility—and a round rustic-cum-modern chandelier are the perfect fit for the curving architecture of the breakfast area. The unobstructed windows maximize the peaceful views of the lake.

Facing Page: Since the lodge room is the first space past the foyer, we draw the eye out toward the lake through a neutral palette and an impressive ceiling treatment crafted with reclaimed pine from old barns. The handsome curved leather sofa maximizes the seating area around the fireplace, and multiple textures animate the room.
Photographs by G. Frank Hart Photography

Above: Hammered copper sinks, hand-glazed tiles, and extended cabinets with lighted nooks impart a sense of grandeur to the family's favorite gathering space. A single-height island is the hub of activity and facilitates interaction with guests while entertaining.

Left: Forgoing the formal atmosphere, we captured a comfortable feel through texture, a bit of color, and multiple fabric prints. The window treatments add textural elements of slubby silk, suede, and natural beads. The distressed, multilayered finishes on the furniture and the large, asymmetrical floral patterns in the rug inject playfulness into the space.

Facing Page: We gave the keeping room a flat hearth and stone surround; it's one of three uniquely designed fireplaces in the home. The blue tones from other spaces continue, but are emphasized with a bright statement rug. Coffers with subtle color inside and additional detailing—like the apothecary drawers in the built-ins and the board and batten above the fireplace—keep the eye moving.
Photographs by G. Frank Hart Photography

Todd Richesin Interiors

One of the pleasures of being an interior designer is helping people develop or hone their sense of style —and then presenting it through their home's interior design. It can sometimes be a challenge to interpret people's preferences, but that challenge is precisely what Todd Richesin loves about his profession. When he's creating tropical retreats, indoor-outdoor connections are a common theme, yet Todd never ceases to surprise with his progressive interpretations of what the locale requires. The designer's mantra is to create homes that are beautiful, comfortable, livable, and fun.

Above & Facing Page: In southern Florida, lounging around by the pool with a good book is a popular form of relaxation, so outdoor living spaces are just as important as a home's interior. I reinterpreted a traditional 1840s Key West conch house to be a bit more refined. All of the interior Dade County pine woodwork was stripped down and repainted in typical Key West fashion. The outdoor draperies have a cooling effect when viewed from the sun-drenched pool, and the line between inside and outside is blurred. Because the owners only use the home a few months out of the year, my goal was to create a true sanctuary, a place where the rest of the world becomes irrelevant the minute they arrive. This is accomplished by the soft color palette, well-edited collections, comfortable furniture, and perfect amount of detailing.
Photographs by Barry Fitzgerald

Above Left & Facing Page Top: Light aqua walls create an ethereal feeling in the bedroom, and a braided rug adds a soft coolness that invites you in for a rest. The Italian secretary hides a television, and mirrored nightstands give a touch of glamour by reflecting the light from the outdoor pool. The connecting bathing area continues the theme of elegance.

Above Right & Facing Page Bottom: You feel the history of the house the moment you walk in the door. I wanted to capitalize on that feeling by incorporating rich, warm fabrics. The giant stylized animals, flowers, and plants on the chocolate background of the draperies are really unexpected for a tropical project. Little details around the room, like the whimsical parakeets on the desk, give you a sense of place but don't weigh the room down. The office is a cozy retreat where the owner can find inspiration to write his great American novel.
Photographs by Barry Fitzgerald

"Collections reflect a well-traveled, well-educated person who has lived an interesting life. This is where the magic happens in interior design." *Todd Richesin*

White Interiors

A room's design connects to the emotions through color, spatial arrangement, and function. Whether it's a bathroom, bedroom, or a formal entertainment area, a room can project a unique emotion. The proper design and arrangement of furnishings are essential to creating an ambience of welcome and comfort. Sherry White refines this concept with her use of clean lines, an uncluttered feel, and a comfortable elegance in each of her designs.

Above: The residents of an oceanfront vacation home preferred a touch of formality but still wanted to experience a comfortable place to relax. I achieved this goal by adding an abundance of color in the living room and adjacent breakfast area with the selection of a floral pattern on the chaise lounges and use of appropriate accessories throughout the room.
Photograph by Roger Squires

Facing Page: After helping select the waterside lot for the home, I was inspired to design the interior as if it were an integral part of the natural environment. Through the use of reclaimed materials—like the flooring from an old warehouse in New York City that was damaged on 9/11 and old sugar molds used as candleholders —the home took on a Low Country feel with a casual yet sophisticated approach. Antiques, like the apothecary chest in the dining room, inhabit nearly every space and speak to function as well as comfort.
Photograph by John McManus

Above: The homeowners of the unique coastal home appreciate 18th-century designs but wanted a more relaxed space for everyday living. A peach strie on the walls paired with a grasscloth table base eases the formal lines of the mahogany tabletop and chairs and helps create a comfortable and elegant blend of styles.
Photograph by Roger Squires

Left & Facing Page Bottom: Balancing the natural undertones of the reclaimed materials while providing modern technological conveniences was an important undertaking. Surrounded by recovered Baltimore cobblestone and a hand-cut wood mantel in the family room, I added a stunning painting that pulls away from the wall to reveal a 42-inch television. Similarly in the master bedroom, another TV is graciously hidden at the foot of the bed, allowing the focus to land on the maple floor and ceiling. Sourced from an old textile mill, the wood received its unique color from the cotton oils and embedded metal shavings, called travelers, which were thrown from the milling machines. Function and beauty are in equal balance throughout this signature home.
Left photograph by Paul Numberg
Facing page bottom photograph by Eric Horan

Facing Page Top: The bedroom immediately makes its visitors feel secure and offers everything a guest could want: an armoire, desk, comfortable chair, great lighting, lined window treatments for privacy, and a connection to the local area through historical artwork. The dropped ceiling color and darker trim animate the simplicity of the room.
Photograph by Ben Ham

Anita Rankin Interiors

During more than 30 years as a designer, Anita Rankin has learned how to optimally use color, whether subtly reflected in an accessory or boldly displayed on a large wall. Combining color with a variety of textures, proper scale, and a seamless connection between rooms, she is well known for creating sophisticated, inviting, and livable homes that reflect the preferences, personalities, and lifestyles of their owners.

Above & Facing Page: The concept for a new home on Mobile Bay began with a pair of antique front doors from a plantation in Lafayette, Louisiana. My goal was to create a beautiful, comfortable home, evoking the atmosphere of an old bay cottage with pine flooring, large mouldings, and 12-foot ceilings while providing spaces designed with functionality and entertainment in mind. A large bayside screened porch just off the living area flawlessly merges indoor and outdoor spaces and allows open access to spectacular waterfront views. To enhance the flow among rooms, I took cues from the bold red color of the kitchen, where the lively pragmatism of the natural gathering space blends with the adjacent comfortable sitting area around a fireplace. In the dining and living rooms, ample seating areas employ varied chair styles and fabrics, including flexible dining table seating for as few as six or as many as 16 guests.
Photographs by Courtland William Richards

Cindy Meador Interiors

Through a combination of her fashion and design knowledge, Cindy Meador has a broad understanding of different styles and influences. This allows her to generate remarkable designs that speak of the genteel area of the South yet are individualized for each homeowner. Incorporating her sources to craft endless possibilities, Cindy's work is unique but not trendy, eclectic but not overstimulating, glamorous but not stuffy. Her final designs are appealing on many levels; whether they're casual, rustic, or coastal, the spaces are sophisticated and distinguished.

Above Left: Following the request of the homeowner, who has a keen sense for color, I imparted a tone-on-tone color palette. A custom rug brings in an animal print without being over the top, and contemporary art punctuates the space. In the summer, the homeowner adds white slipcovers to the furniture so the colorful accessories truly pop.

Above Right: Ono Island is a majestic place that is unhurried and unspoiled—perfect for a vacation residence. The mix of clean, streamlined color next to the more rustic table makes for an unexpected surprise. The gorgeous view married with the soothing colors enforce a serene, floating atmosphere.

Facing Page: The retreat's location directly next to the water prompted the ocean theme for the master bedroom. A local artist and friend of the homeowner painted the beautiful artwork, which simply made the entire room pop. I paired the contemporary art with a rug design that mimicks waves and sand-like colors on the furniture to visually bring the sea inside.
Photographs by Parish Stapleton

Design Lines

The creativity of interior design is not contained in the typical 9-to-5 job; instead, a good designer is always on the lookout for fresh ideas. Judy Pickett, FASID, takes this theory to heart. Every space, form, and color—especially those inherent in nature—provide her with a source of inspiration. First pulled into the design industry by fashion and a love affair with textiles, Judy quickly realized the impact designers have on their clients. In partnership with five fabulous designers, Judy funnels her expertise and inspiration into creating spaces that make a difference in people's lives.

Above & Facing Page: Upon meeting the exuberant, multigenerational, Italian family who would live in the five-story home, I knew that the palette and furnishings would need to be neutral to allow their personalities to come to life. Simple black baseboards and window trim frame the rooms and allow the tremendous water views to take precedence. To accommodate the family's sophisticated taste, rustic elegance was achieved with beautiful, stucco-like wall treatments, flatweave rugs, and limestone floors. Overall, the project—which we were involved with from the blueprint stage to the final picture hanging—resulted in a refined, understated Tuscan feel that exudes the life that is evident in the family.
Photographs by Philip Beaurline

Knotting Hill Interiors

Timeless elegance is an essential quality to any thoughtfully designed space, along with breathtaking beauty, innovation, and great ideas. At Knotting Hill Interiors, where Kimberly Grigg is founder and principal designer, timelessness often is reflected through the use of quirky, potentially trendy items that are juxtaposed in a classic setting. Elegance is a little more ethereal, but Kimberly thoughtfully achieves the appropriate level through careful layering of textiles, accessories, furniture, and art. By absorbing the homeowner's personality, preferences, and lifestyle, Kimberly defines each space as an expression of life and beauty that will withstand the test of time.

Above: Every selection and concept for a newly renovated home focused on eco-friendliness, as well as beauty, because the family embraces the green movement. In partnership with the architect and builder, we wasted nothing, even creating an outdoor fireplace mantel from a tree root that was removed for the home's new footprint. Most of the furnishings were made of reclaimed materials, including the table and chairs in the kitchen. Above the table, a vintage phone from the couple's early years hangs under a plaque from an old telephone booth in England, where the husband's family originates.

Facing Page: The home's soft, muted tones—which mimic a favorite piece of art—suit the family members' personalities and their desire for a peaceful, elegant ambience. The relatively unadorned reclaimed table and antique buffet reflect calmness, as does the simple cotton velvet drapery. I found a local artisan to hand-paint birds on the linen chair backs, adding a cotton skirt for a bit of subtle drama.
Photographs by Matt Silk Photographics

index

INTERIORS

SOUTHEAST TEAM

ASSOCIATE PUBLISHER: Emily Timotheo

GRAPHIC DESIGNER: Paul Strength

EDITOR: Jennifer Nelson

PRODUCTION COORDINATOR: Drea Williams

HEADQUARTERS TEAM

PUBLISHER: Brian G. Carabet

PUBLISHER: John A. Shand

EXECUTIVE PUBLISHER: Phil Reavis

PUBLICATION & CIRCULATION MANAGER: Lauren B. Castelli

SENIOR GRAPHIC DESIGNER: Emily A. Kattan

MANAGING EDITOR: Rosalie Z. Wilson

EDITOR: Anita M. Kasmar

EDITOR: Sarah Tangney

EDITOR: Lindsey Wilson

MANAGING PRODUCTION COORDINATOR: Kristy Randall

PROJECT COORDINATOR: Laura Greenwood

ADMINISTRATIVE MANAGER: Carol Kendall

CLIENT SUPPORT COORDINATOR: Amanda Mathers

PANACHE PARTNERS, LLC
CORPORATE HEADQUARTERS
1424 Gables Court
Plano, TX 75075
469.246.6060
www.panache.com
www.panachedesign.com

Carolyn Hultman Interior Design, page 216

THE PANACHE COLLECTION

CREATING SPECTACULAR PUBLICATIONS FOR DISCERNING READERS

Dream Homes Series
An Exclusive Showcase of the Finest Architects, Designers and Builders

Carolinas
Chicago
Coastal California
Colorado
Deserts
Florida
Georgia
Los Angeles
Metro New York
Michigan
Minnesota
New England

New Jersey
Northern California
Ohio & Pennsylvania
Pacific Northwest
Philadelphia
South Florida
Southwest
Tennessee
Texas
Washington, D.C.

Spectacular Homes Series
An Exclusive Showcase of the Finest Interior Designers

California
Carolinas
Chicago
Colorado
Florida
Georgia
Heartland
London
Michigan
Minnesota
New England

Metro New York
Ohio & Pennsylvania
Pacific Northwest
Philadelphia
South Florida
Southwest
Tennessee
Texas
Toronto
Washington, D.C.
Western Canada

Perspectives on Design Series
Design Philosophies Expressed by Leading Professionals

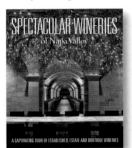

California
Carolinas
Chicago
Colorado
Florida
Georgia
Great Lakes
London

Minnesota
New England
New York
Pacific Northwest
South Florida
Southwest
Western Canada

Art of Celebration Series
The Making of a Gala

Chicago & the Greater Midwest
Georgia
New England
New York
Northern California
South Florida
Southern California
Southern Style
Southwest
Toronto
Washington, D.C.

Spectacular Wineries Series
A Captivating Tour of Established, Estate and Boutique Wineries

California's Central Coast
Napa Valley
New York
Sonoma County
Texas

Experience Series
The Most Interesting Attractions, Hotels, Restaurants, and Shops

Boston
British Columbia
Chicago
Denver
Southern California
Twin Cities

City by Design Series
An Architectural Perspective

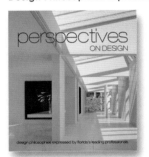

Atlanta
Charlotte
Chicago
Dallas
Denver
Orlando
Phoenix
San Francisco
Texas

Specialty Titles
The Finest in Unique Luxury Lifestyle Publications

21st Century Homes
Cloth and Culture: Couture Creations of Ruth E. Funk
Distinguished Inns of North America
Extraordinary Homes California
Geoffrey Bradfield Ex Arte
Into the Earth: A Wine Cave Renaissance
Shades of Green Tennessee
Spectacular Golf of Colorado
Spectacular Golf of Texas
Spectacular Hotels
Spectacular Restaurants of Texas
Visions of Design

Panache Books App
Inspiration at Your Fingertips

Download the Panache Books app in the iTunes Store to access the digital version of Interiors Southeast and other Panache Partners publications. Each book offers inspiration at your fingertips.

PanacheDesign.com
Where the Design Industry's Finest Professionals Gather, Share, and Inspire

PanacheDesign.com overflows with innovative ideas from leading architects, builders, interior designers, and other specialists. A gallery of design photographs and library of advice-oriented articles are among the comprehensive site's offerings.

Panache Partners, LLC   1424 Gables Court   Plano, Texas 75075   469.246.6060   www.panache.com